MW01147762

West Tampa Stories

Volume 1

copyright 2010

Author, Editor and Layout

Fred Tomasello Jr.

For information on contacting the author, write or email:

Fred Tomasello Jr.
53 Harmony Lane
Cheektowaga NY 14225

fredt2929@aol.com

Angie and Fred Tomasello, my Ma and Dad

Nana Angelina, me and Dad at 2609 St. Conrad

TABLE OF CONTENTS

St. Joseph Catholic School   5

Bless Me Father, For I Have Sinned   11

Argelio Morales & My Big Fight   23

First Love   39

Throwing Eggs   61

What Happened to Lastra's Pharmacy?   105

Wayne Bright, Us Against Them   111

Ralph Lavandera and Nellie Fox's Bat   115

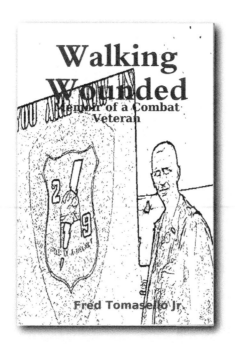

Walking Wounded: Memoir of a Combat Veteran

by

Fred Tomasello Jr.

Available from the author or from Lulu.com.

Fred served three years as an officer in the US Marine Corps earning two Purple Hearts, five Air Medals and a heavy dose of Post Traumatic Stress. "Walking Wounded" is a look at the life of an Infantry Platoon Commander, Aerial Observer and Casualty Assistance Officer as well as the long-term effects of war on a persons' life and family.

Born and raised in West Tampa, Fred graduated from USF and worked 27 years at the Tampa Post Office, retiring in 1999. He and his wife Kathy Blair "snow-bird" every winter from Cheektowaga NY were Fred writes about issues affecting veterans.

St. Joseph Catholic School

Ma and Dad sent me to St. Joseph's on Albany near Cherry Street. Every day I walked home from school wearing navy blue pants and white shirt, announcing to all the public school kids that I went to Catholic School. We were dismissed from school later in the afternoon so the streets were filled with kids already out and playing for the afternoon. Every time I walked in front of Ricky Leto's house, he was always sitting on his porch on a steel rocking chair, looking out over the street. We usually stared at each other and then one of us would call the other a name, like, "You Bird!"

Ricky would leap off his chair, run down the porch steps and jump me, knocking me to the ground. I would try to fight but Ricky always beat me up--always. Crying, I'd walk into my house, my white shirt dirty, sometimes with a button popped out, and tell my mother. Ma would stand me up on the top of the toilet seat, wash my bruises and change my clothes.

"Fight back," she'd tell me, "punch him in the nose and he'll stop picking on you."

I never did punch Ricky Leto in the nose and after many fights we became friends, both of us knowing that he could beat me up anytime he wanted.

St Joseph School was across the street from St. Joseph Church, both on Albany Avenue. The routine every morning involved Ma and Dad leaving me at church where I went inside for mass. All of us kids gathered in the church and when mass was over, we went outside and lined up by class so the nuns could march us across the street into the school.

The nuns who ran St. Joseph were Salesian Sisters and they wore black veils that came down to their waists in the back, black habits with long sleeves that were wide enough to allow the nuns to pin them up so they could work with their hands and arms without constraint. The habits were drawn in around the waist with some kind of rope around which hung a large rosary complete with a big cross with Jesus nailed onto it. The habit went down below their ankles almost covering their black leather shoes that wrapped tightly around their feet and reached up to the middle of their calves. I saw their covered calves once when a nun played kick-ball with us and hiked up her gown to be able to run and kick the ball. Everything they wore was black except for starched white cloth that covered their foreheads, went down the sides of their faces, covered their ears, and buttoned under their chins, protecting their necks. Around their necks they wore a large white starch bib that covered the front of their chests. The bib was always kept immaculately clean and stiffly starched.

Each morning after mass, we assembled on the side of the church and Sister Francis, our first grade teacher, would walk us across the street, through the playground, into the school, and up the steps to our classrooms on the second floor. The first floor held the cafeteria and some offices for the Mother Superior, the second floor held classrooms for first, second and third grades, and the third floor for fourth through eighth grades. Both the church and school were built completely out of wood and everything creaked when we walked upon the old boards.

The old wooden church was infested with termites and the parish was too poor to repair the damage so we all just lived with the termites. Father Brown was offering the mass one Sunday morning and during the elevation, when he raised the chalice filled with wine up over his head, a winged termite, so fat he could not fly, fell from the ceiling and plunked into the wine. Without hesitation, Father Brown put the chalice to his lips and chugged until the chalice was empty, swallowing the termite in the process. After mass outside, everyone was around him and he was laughing about the termite saying, "What could I do, the termite was blessed. I couldn't throw it away, so I drank it down, a holy termite."

Sister Francis, my first grade teacher was very nice. One day I was sitting next to a boy named Ronald DeBoo and he swung his fist around and punched me right on the nose. Blood poured onto my white shirt while Sister Francis scolded Ronald and asked him why he punched me. Ronald frowned and stared at Sister Francis and then he stared at me. My nose hurt but my heart hurt even more because I had done nothing to provoke this punch and wondered why people could hurt someone else for no reason at all. This went completely against the church and God's teachings. I ruined many white shirts during my times at St. Joseph Catholic School.

Each successive year, the nuns became stricter and more violent. In the third grade, Sister Jerome was the worst. Each student was required to have a fountain pen, ruler, pencil and ink bottle on top of their desk at all times. Whenever we did something wrong, she would grab the nearest ruler, run up to you and tell you to hold out your hand, palm up. Then she would squeeze your fingers with one hand and whip your hand with the ruler until you began to cry. If the whole class needed to be punished, she would line us up in front of the desks, side by side and we would hold out both hands, palms up. She would begin on one end of the line and smack each palm once or twice as she went down the line. Sometimes we'd keep one hand behind our backs and just put out one hand, receiving only half of a beating. To our great surprise, the nun never noticed. Maybe it was indicative of how anger blinds a person or perhaps the violence she was inflicting pricked her conscience to the extent that she overlooked our humble attempts to mitigate her wrath.

In the fourth grade, when I was 10 years old, a new student transferred to our class. His name was William Agear. Never had we seen such a boy get into trouble so fast. He was the first person I remember to ever use the word "fuck" in nearly every sentence, out loud and in front of anyone.

At recess, we were usually out in the playground throwing acorns at each other. One day we stopped and watched Father Brown leave the priest's rectory next door to the church, climb into his car and drive away. We always treated Father Brown with respect and awe. He was a tall, heavy, priest who was quite old, had big jowls, a blotched complexion, flimsy strands of white hair and wheezed, opening and closing his lips with each gasp like a huge grouper out of water, laying on the bottom of a boat and suffocating to death. In addition to respect, I felt sorry for Father Brown because of his age and his physical condition.

William Agear stared at Father Brown until the car door closed.

"He's a fat fucker, isn't he? I'll bet he fucks all the nuns," William spoke in a voice loud enough for the whole playground to hear. Everyone stopped playing and looked in horror at William who enjoyed the attention.

"Mister, Mister, don't fuck me," he sang out loud. "Fuck Sister Antoinette behind the tree!"

Shocked and speechless, I stared at William Agear, expecting a lightning bolt to strike him dead and knowing he must run to confession or die with a severe, dirty stain on his soul sending him to the depths of hell for eternity.

On another day, when I got up the courage, I asked him about the word "fuck" and what it meant.

"That's how your mother and father made you," he laughed. "By fucking."

I could sense it was a bad word and I already had soap put in my mouth for saying bad words so I tried never to say that word in front of adults or girls because I didn't want to get in trouble. I was interested in how I was made and pondered what "fucking" meant and what that had to do with making children.

In the fifth grade, my last year at St. Joseph, I misbehaved one day and had to go to the convent where the nuns lived. They forced us to work there, doing manual labor like pulling weeds outside, sweeping the inside and doing other odd jobs.

I asked the nun if I could go to the bathroom and she said no so I ran away, went home and told my mother and father. They went to the school and complained and the next year I was finally out of Catholic school and enrolled in public school.

I went half a year to Cuesta Elementary and the other half at Mitchell Elementary while Dad built our house on Nassau Street. I never had to open a book because we already learned what they were teaching.

The next year I looked forward to attending West Tampa Junior High School, the "Fighting Greyhounds!"

Dad and I in front of our first house, the partially completed Jim Walter Home at 2610 St. John St.

Bless Me Father, For I Have Sinned

I must get to Heaven.

Sister Jerome wears a white piece of cloth over her chest, starched stiff, that looks like a bib. She compares that cloth to our souls.

"Only when your soul is pure and white, like this cloth, will you be allowed to enter Heaven. Just one tiny mark, one little stain and you'll be barred from Heaven. You'll be sent to Purgatory or Hell where you will burn in horrendous pain without dying until enough people pray for you to get you out, usually several years or more.

"In the back of your missals are prayers called 'plenary indulgences' that are worth periods of time depending on the length and power of the prayer. I recommend you recite those prayers, many times over. Indulgences are accumulated or banked until you die and then credited against your years in Purgatory. If you have enough of them banked, you can cancel Purgatory and reroute your soul directly to Heaven."

For days, I recite these prayers over and over again, hundreds of times, until I have thousands of years worth of plenary indulgences in case I die with a venial sin on my soul.

"The Catholic church also sells plenary indulgences," Sister Jerome tells us. "Your family can buy a mass for the repose of your soul in Purgatory."

Forget that. My family is so poor I can't count on anybody paying my way out of hell.

"Heaven," Sister Jerome smiles, "is where we all want to go. It's beautiful. Filled with martyrs, angels and saints. Your relatives and friends who died without sin are there too. So are your favorite pets and other wonderful things. You can see God and Jesus whenever you wish."

One day Sister Jerome asked each of us what we wished for most in the world. No matter what we answered, she said we'd find it in Heaven. Bicycles, clothes, dolls, money, everything, was already up there waiting for us.

When she got to me all I could think of that I wanted, without copying someone else, was "spaghetti and meat balls."

Everyone laughed.

"Shut up!" Sister Jerome barked. "Yes, Freddie. Plenty. All you have to do in Heaven is just think of spaghetti and meatballs and a plate full appears right in front of you, ready to eat. And all you have to do to get to Heaven is to make a good, honest, complete and full confession."

A few days later, Sister Jerome surprised me by chasing me down and catching me in the schoolyard during recess. How could I have known she was quick as a panther under that black robe.

Honeybees entered the Hibiscus buds and us boys would pinch off the opening, trapping the bee inside. Then we would yank the buds off the bush and jam the bloom containing the bee down each other's backs. Kids screamed in panic. Holding me by pinching my ear, Sister Jerome pulled me inside the classroom, grabbed a ruler and furiously smacked the palm of my hand over and over again until the ruler shattered. Instead of the usual wooden rulers we were required to have on our desks, she blindly grabbed one of those new, expensive plastic rulers and it splintered into pieces as I cried, my feet churning in pain and my eyes squeezed shut against the shrapnel assaulting my face.

She never smiled at me again.

Sister Jerome taught catechism every day and her comments were aimed directly at me. She was preparing us for our First Confession and Communion.

"The only way to enter Heaven is to die with a pure, clean, soul," she stressed, "a soul free from sin. Martyrs are the only exception. If you die as a martyr for Jesus Christ and the Catholic Church, put to death by enemies of the church, like in a war, martyrs go straight to Heaven."

All the nuns told us stories about Communism and how people were tortured for their religious beliefs. Nuns were killed if they refused to denounce their faith in God. Priests had their thumb, index and ring fingers amputated so they could not pick up a host and offer Holy Communion.

We Catholics believed that the host, when conse-crated in the mass, became the body and blood of Jesus Christ, not symbolically, but actually and physically, an everyday miracle of the Church.
Sister Jerome told us communist soldiers once laid a Communion wafer on top of a steel anvil and pounded the host with a hammer. Blood ran and the soldiers fell to their knees begging the priests to forgive them.

"Now, what are sins?" Sister Jerome continued, staring right at me. "Venial sins are the 'little' sins, the ones you commit without intent or without understanding the seriousness of the sin. If you die with just one little venial sin on your soul, you are going to Purgatory for hundreds of years. Purgatory is a horrible waiting station between Heaven and Hell. You suffer and burn in Purgatory, just like Hell, but there's a chance you can get out and go to Heaven--if people pray for you.

"A mortal sin, on the other hand, is a sin so evil that it results in a complete loss of grace. Mortal sin equals eternal damnation. In Hell. Forever.

"Breaking one of the ten commandments or any commandment of the church is a mortal sin. You will pay. For example, if you eat meat on Friday, it's a mortal sin. And if you die, you're doomed to Hell for eternity. No possible chance of salvation."

Outside the open window, a butterfly flits by.

"Quit looking out the window, Freddie. Pay attention! Everyone! The only way to have your sins absolved or forgiven is through the sacrament of Penance. This means a good and perfect confession followed by a sincere Act of Contrition. Then you must recite the prayers for Penance that the priest gives you. They're necessary before God will forgive your sins."

Sister Jerome also taught about death.

"There are so many ways you can die, Freddie. Some are unexpected and quick. You could be struck by a car crossing the street or riding your bike; get a cramp swimming in deep water and drown; struck by lightning playing outside; you could crash in an auto accident, suffer a brain tumor, stroke, cancer, Tuberculosis, or some other serious illness. You could be murdered, strangled or shot by a maniac on your way home from school. You never know when or why."

First Confession day finally arrives. All of us are in lines, straight orderly lines, boys in navy blue pants and white shirts on one wall of the church, girls in navy blue skirts and white blouses on the other side. The empty church feels quiet and strange as we examine our consciences. My shoulders slump and I exhale, long and deep. The floorboards creak when I shift my skinny body from one foot to another, probably because of the weight of all my sins. I've got to remember each sin and how many times I committed them. Hitting others and making others cry are easy sins to remember. Some acts I'm not so sure about, like sins of "omission and commission." Then there's lies, missing church, and finally, the sin that gets me every time, the thought of sinning. I can't control my thoughts. Sister Jerome said that just thinking about violence or impurity is a sin.

Across the church at the girls' line they're concentrating, heads bowed. The boys are too. Even the jokers are afraid. Everyone looks serious.

As each child leaves the curtained confessional, they walk to the front of the church and kneel down in the pew nearest to the altar to say their penance. Sitting one row behind is Sister Jerome herself.

There are just two boys in front of me now. I mentally review my sins. God, I should have written them down so I could make sure none get left out but I was afraid someone would find my list and squeal on me. Now, with my luck, any little sin I forget to mention won't be absolved and I'll be doomed to hell.

The boy in front of me walks into the confessional. I'm next. My heart pounds as fear floods over me. Who'll be the priest? God, I hope he doesn't recognize me or know my parents. Slim chance of that. What if my sins are so shameful he stops, kicks me out and won't give me absolution? What if he gives me so many prayers to recite that I forget one? I'll be damned to Hell forever.

What's taking so long? He's been in there longer than anyone else. Is the priest giving him a long talk?

Calm down. Get ready.

Oh God, I'm next.

Finally, the boy marches out and I part the curtains and walk in, making sure they close behind me and kneel down. In front of my face is a little screened window. As I bow my head, strong feelings of shame flood over me. I make the sign of the cross with my right hand and my voice cracks as I begin.

"In the name of the Father, and of the Son, and of the Holy Ghost, Amen. Bless me Father, for I have sinned. This is my first confession and these are my sins."

Long pause. With a loud gulp, I whisper.

"Once I ate meat on Friday. I was eating at a friend's house and his parents served beef stew. They weren't Catholic and I was afraid to tell them that I couldn't eat meat on Fridays, so I ate it.

"I hit my sister many times and made her cry. Well, no, I mean, I just hit her once and that makes her cry. But I do it every day . . . well, sometimes two or three times a day. Every time I hit her, Father, she cries and tells my mom and dad and then they hit me. I don't hit her many times but sometimes I do. Usually once is enough, you know, like a good punch in the arm or I smack the back of her head, like a slap, and she always starts to cry. Now, all I gotta do is raise my hand like I'm going to hit her and she starts crying.

"Once I was playing with matches and started a rag on fire at my Grandmother's house. The rag burned up and caught a wooden post on fire and soon my Grandmother's back porch caught fire. I got a good beating that day, first from my uncle and later from my Dad when he got home from work.

"I've spoken God's name in vain several times . . . well, maybe hundreds of times. Like when I'm trying to nail something and the hammer hits my finger. Or when I'm playing baseball and strike out or make an error.

"I've also lied many times so I won't get in trouble with my mom and dad. Like, I lie about playing with firecrackers 'cause I'm not supposed to or playing with water moccasins down by the creek.

"Oh yeah, I'm not sure if this is a sin but it might be. Me and my friend Pepe, we throw rocks at the roof of this old lady's house. She has a tin roof and we throw them from behind his shed so she can't see us. Pepe has a whole dump truck pile of white rocks there so we can throw about six or seven of them high in the air before the first one hits her roof. We keep throwing them until she screams. Pepe's mother told us that the old lady's a witch so we do this every afternoon after school, even if it's raining. If she is a witch, I don't think it's a sin, but I'm confessing it just in case. One time the old lady's son came over and talked to Pepe's mother so we stopped for a while. Now we only do it once a week. I told Pepe I can't do it anymore, especially after this first confession, because it feels like a sin. I'm pretty sure it's a sin.

"Many of my friends are richer than we are and they have things that I want. Sometimes I wish they would die so I could get their bike or new baseball glove, or football.

"When I get real mad at them, I wish I could kill them or I wish they would die right in front of me, like from a terrible accident, so I could enjoy watching them die. I've even wished this about my sister; and my mother and father. Sometimes I even see'em dead and in their coffins."

At this point, I pause and shudder. Another huge wave of shame showers me from head to toe. What must this priest think? I wait a moment or two, expecting to hear something from the priest, a grunt of disgust, some words of disapproval and condemnation, anything.

I hear nothing.

If this were Sister Jerome, just one of these sins reaching her ears would result in several hours of talking filled with hell and damnation.

Still hearing nothing, I guess the priest wants me to go on. Maybe he's used to this sort of thing. My voice croaks over what I have to confess next.

"Father, sometimes I play with myself down there. I can't help it, especially at night when it's dark and I can't get to sleep. I also think impure thoughts about girls. I've done this many times, almost every night.

"Once, I was playing with the girl who lives across the street from my Grandmother's. We hid behind the mango tree to play doctor. She laid on a little bench and I pretended to give her a shot with a mango leaf. I begged her to take her pants down and her underpants off so I could give her a shot in her butt. Finally she took them off and I saw all of her. Then I took off my pants and she saw all of me and gave me a shot in the bottom. I think of her at nights, impure thoughts, and then I play with myself. I've done this with her twice. The last time, her mother caught us and now she's not allowed to play with me anymore.

"At Alonzo's drug store, when no one's looking, I open up magazines with naked women in them. I put the magazine inside a comic book so people think I'm reading the comic book. I've done this many times, about twice a week, every week for over a year.

"When I see girls or women dressed up in a way that shows their tops or bottoms, I get impure thoughts. I try to resist them by praying the Hail Mary or Our Father, but these thoughts just keep popping into my mind. This happens a lot, almost every day, Father, and I keep trying to quit but I can't."

I pause.

"Father, I can't think of any more sins."

Another long pause.

"Uh, that's all, Father. What do I do now?"

"Father, I'm sorry for all my sins. I'm ready to make an act of contrition."

"Father . . . Father?"

Sister Jerome told us that after we finished, the Priest would have a few words to say to us, tell us what prayers we had to say for Penance, and then he would listen to us recite our Act of Contrition.

I hear nothing.

Leaning closer, I stare at the screen and try to peer through the mesh to see if I could recognize which priest is in there. I can't see anything. Sweat rolls down my forehead and my armpits, tickling the sides of my chest.

What's going on? Why isn't he answering me? Is he so horrified he's can't speak? He's shocked, scared to death that God's going to strike us down, right here, right now, inside this confessional. He can't say anything because he's so ashamed of me.

My brain goes numb. I squeeze my eyes shut.

The sound of a tiny doorknob startles me. I open my eyes and a small door behind the screen squeaks opens in front of my face. The light inside is bright, but I can't see the priest's face or recognize the shape of his head.

Confused, ashamed, and frightened, I just stare.

After a few moments, the priest says, "OK, I'm ready. You can begin your confession."

"But, uhh, I've already made my confession, Father."

"Well, you have to do it again. I didn't hear you."

Suddenly I realize that only one priest takes turns listening to the two lines of boys and girls. Sister Jerome never said that. This explains why everyone takes so long. I thought two priests were inside the confessional, one for each line and also to give each other moral support while listening to our horrible sins. God, I screwed this up.

Shaking and shivering in the hot confessional, I try to remember and repeat my sins. Nervous, I stutter and forget many.

Afterwards, the priest mumbles something about avoiding the near occasion of sin, tells me to pray every day and for my penance, he wants me to say ten Our Fathers, ten Hail Mary's and ten Glory Be's. Then he tells me to make a good Act of Contrition.

Right in the middle I forget the words. The priest helps me get through it and I stumble out of the confessional, walk to the front of the church and kneel down in front of Sister Jerome.

Unable to stop myself, I turn around and look at her. She already knows, probably from the look on my face, that I've really messed up my first confession. She glances left and right, reaches over, pinches my ear and yanks hard until the back of my head bangs against the pew. The pain brings tears to my eyes and I start to cry. She puts her blurry face an inch in front of mine and our noses nearly touch. Helpless and frozen with fear, I look deep into Sister Jerome's eyes as she hisses at me.

"You better pray as hard as you can, Freddie. You're evil. And you're going to Hell. Straight to Hell."

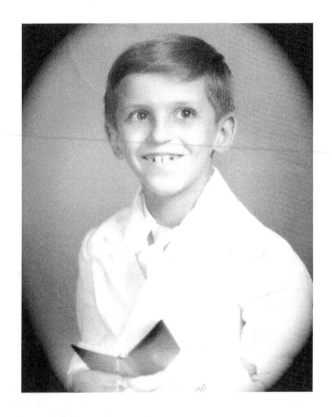

Perhaps this child wasn't as angelic as he looked.

Argelio Morales & My Big Fight

"Ooh, have you seen the new guy? He's really cute."

"He's from Spain. Moved to Tampa during the Christmas holidays. What a way to start the new year! Hooray, 1959!"

"He's learning English. I'll be glad to teach him."

"His name is Argelio Morales. Look! look! There he is. He's finally in school today."

Monday. Tuesday. And now Wednesday. Every day since New Years, all the girls at West Tampa Junior High are chattering over the new guy.

Enough already. What the hell's wrong with these girls? Can't they be satisfied with guys right under their noses? Guys like me? I'm available. Why don't they like me?

Argelio Morales. What the hell kind of a name is that? Sounds like some Spanish song. Wonder if he's related to "Johnny Boy" Morales who's in reform school now, in Marianna, Florida. Good old Johnny Boy. Little man, big *cojones*. Tough little bastard, never backed down from anybody. A West Tampa legend. Balls bigger than his brain, though. Guess that's why he's in jail. Wonder how tough this Argelio is. Damn those girls.

What the hell, it's January, 1959 and I'm a ninth grader just like I should be, not like a lot of these hoodlums who've flunked two or three times. Big, tough guys. Get their pick of the girls, though. Take 'em out in their cars, scare 'em, get 'em pregnant, then leave 'em.

"We got our own four 'F' club," they say, "just like the cracker farmers. "'Find 'em, feel 'em, fuck 'em and forget 'em.' Ha-ha-ha."

Bums, all of 'em. Hey, I even got a job, soda jerking at Lastra's Pharmacy, fifty cents an hour. Lots'a money in my pockets now. And I brush my teeth twice a day. Think these girls would notice? Oh, no. I'm not good enough for them. They go for some foreign greaser who can't even speak English. Hell, I'm trilingual. I can order food in English, Spanish and Italian--cafe con leche, media noches, Paella, Ropa Vieja, Boliche, empanadas, and my all-time favorite, jaiba enchilada.

What the hell else do these girls want?

Stupid asses. All of 'em.

Let me check this guy out. Hell, he's not hard to find. Just look for a gaggle of goofy girls practicing their Spanish. There he is.

Argelio is three inches taller than me, new clothes, dark curly hair, barbershop trimmed, and he speaks Spanish with some sort of lisp.

"What's he got, Nancy, some kind of speech problem?"

"No, Freddie, he's from Spain, stupid. They speak Castilian, and that's the way they pronounce their words. It's different from the Spanish we speak. Isn't he cute? He looks sooo strong, too."

"Shut up. You're getting me sick. He sounds like a sissy to me."

Oh boy, I can't wait till phys ed today. We're still playing football. I'll make sure he's not on my team, knock the hell out of him a couple of times and see just how tough this guy really is.

At 10:15, the bell rings and all the 9th grade boys go to the locker room to change into our red shorts, white tee shirts and tennis shoes. Argelio doesn't have red shorts. He comes out in a black bathing suit, the short tight ones like professional wrestlers wear, no shirt and bare footed. What a dumb ass. His legs and chest are so white he looks like a queer. I hope he steps on sand spurs.

"You know the routine, boys," Coach Urso says as he throws out a football. "LaRussa, Roses, you're captains today."

"Sir, its Rosas," Julio says. "R-O-S-A-S. My name is Julio Rosas. Roses are flowers."

"Shut up, you little asshole. Who's the teacher here? Who's the college grad? You pick teams and play till I blow the whistle. Then come in, shower and get the hell out'a here before the next bell rings. You got 45 minutes. No fighting and no pissing in the shower. I'll be in my office. If I have to come out, somebody's getting their little ass paddled."

Tony LaRussa picks Argelio fifth, trying to be nice and polite to the new guy. Nodding to Julio, I get picked next and can't wait to bust his white ass. A couple of plays into the game, I realize he's never played American football. He takes a few steps, looks around puzzled and jumps out of people's way when they come to block him. He seems to be studying the game as he plays, trying to figure out what to do.

"Julio, run around left end. I'll block for you. I wanna knock the new guy on his ass," I say.

Running a sweep left, I see Argelio fending off a block from someone else. His back is to me and I hit him full speed, throwing my left elbow as hard as I can between his shoulder blades with perfect timing.

Argelio goes flying, tumbles down, does some sort of fancy gymnastic somersault and is back up on his feet in a second. He glares at me. I turn away and trot back to my huddle, acting like nothing happened.

Julio calls a pass play and I stay behind to block. Looking to my right to block a pass rusher, someone creams me from behind, sending me flying. I hit the ground and skid several feet, my face and nose plowing a painful furrow through the sandy grass.

"Clipping, damn it! Clipping! That's clipping, you idiot!" I scream as I roll over onto my back.

Argelio smiles and extends his hand down to help me up. Tony is standing next to him, grinning.

"Hey, Fred, you clipped Argelio first," Tony says. "And we didn't call it. What's fair is fair. You're even now. No more clipping. Get up and shake hands with him."

Pissed at everyone, I ignore his outstretched hand and we play until Coach's whistle blows.

A couple of weeks later, the sport changes to basketball. It's Tuesday and we're out on the concrete court playing skins against shirts. The game is tense because the score is tied and there's only a few minutes left before coach will blow the whistle.

An older guy in street clothes is standing on the sidelines watching us play. The basketball is slapped out of bounds and flies into the guy's hands. He stands there holding the ball and looking at us.

"Hey, throw it here. Come on. Throw it here," I yell.

He ignores me, tucks the ball under his arm, and stares at me. He looks a couple of years older than us, has dark bushy side burns, needs a shave and his hair is slicked back in a greasy pompadour. His collar is raised up behind his neck, classic hoodlum style.

"You want the ball? You come here and take it away from me," he finally says.

"Just throw me the ball, man, we're in the middle of a game."

He smirks, looks around, then looks at me. Everyone stops talking and walk towards us, forming a circle.

"Hey, man, just gimme the ball so we can finish the game. I don't want no trouble," I say. "We're tied and the whistle's about to blow."

"You want this ball? Take it away from me," he says. "You don't have the balls. You a *maricone* boy. No *cojones*. Just a skinny little *pindejo*. You want this ball? Fight me. If any of you other *pindejos* want this ball, you can fight me too. OK?"

We're standing face to face now, barely a foot apart. His breath smells like cigarette smoke and his eyes are black and feverish. He has one bushy eyebrow, a thick, wavy "M," across both his eyes. His dark skin

is zit free, like pimples fear him or maybe he's out-
grown the scourge. When he smirks, a silver tooth
glints in the sun.

"Look, man," I say, "I'm not afraid of you. It's
just that I don't wanna get in trouble fighting here at
school, you know."

"OK. Fine," he answers. "We fight somewhere else.
Friday. 3:30. After school. The field in back of the
Santa Ella Cigar factory. If you're not there, you
prove to everybody you a maricone; no cojones; a yellow
little chicken; a coward."

A referee's whistle shrills loudly. Coach Urso
trots towards us.

"First day back, Dido, and you starting trouble already?" Coach Urso says, his voice deeper than usual.
"Phys ed's over, boys. Break it up and get out'a here."

Julio walks me to the showers.

"That's Dido, man, Dido!" Julio starts. "Don't you
know him? He's the biggest hood in West Tampa! He's
been in reform school. Marianna. Twice. Next time up,
he goes to Raiford with the adults. Everybody's scared
of him, man. And you agreed to fight Dido Friday after
school? He's gonna beat the living shit out of you,
Freddie. Why didn't you just let him keep the damn
ball. Man, I really feel sorry for you. You let him
throw his balls at you in front of everybody, and
worse, you threw yours back at him. You're crazy, man,
and stupid too."

By the 3:30 bell, the whole school is buzzing about
the big fight, everybody.

"Did you hear? Friday. After school, 3:30. Santa Ella cigar factory. Freddie fights Dido. Ha! More like, Dido beats the shit out'a Freddie. He's gonna get slaughtered."

Walking home, my head is down as I think. What can I do? If I chicken out and don't show up, the whole school will know I'm a coward. They'll make fun of me behind my back, even to my face. Especially all the girls. They already don't like me. When they find out I chickened out, not one of them will even talk to me, much less ever go out with me. And if I do show up, he's gonna beat me to a pulp.

I hear footsteps coming up behind me, walking quickly.

Dammit! It's probably Dido. He can't wait till Friday. Gonna kick my ass right now. I turn and it's Argelio Morales, a huge smile on his face.

"Que cojones tu tiene, flaco!" *What big balls you have, skinny.* He's actually dancing around, snapping his wrist, fingers popping like he just struck them with a hammer. "Tu sabe fajar? Si no, yo te enseno." *You know how to fight? If you don't, I'll teach you.*

"Get the hell away from me, man. I'm in deep trouble."

Argelio persists. He tells me he boxed in Spain and works in a gym at the Rosa Valdez Settlement, a church-school mission between West Tampa and the colored section. Tampa is split three ways. The whites, or "Crackers" as we Latinos call them, the colored, and then us, the "spics" as they call us. Spanish and Italian cultures are different, but since we're socially and physically lumped together by the other two groups, we're forced to get along pretty well.

"Yo sabe el secreto para ganar." *I know the secret to winning.*

This gets my attention. I stop walking. What the hell have I got to lose, anyway.

"OK, what's the secret?" I ask.

"Manana, a Rosa Valdez. Yo te enseno."

We agree to meet at the settlement tomorrow after school where he will teach me the secret to winning this fight.

After school the next day, Wednesday, I go directly to Rosa Valdez.

Pa-ke-ta. Pa-ke-ta. Pa-ke-ta. Pa-ke-ta.

Argelio is working a speed bag, standing straight up, chin out, every curly hair exactly in place.

Scientific boxing is sissy fighting. Look at him, posing up there, tapping that little bag, wearing leather mittens. The bag can't punch back. Does he know how stupid he looks? He stops and grins at me, ear to ear. What a dumb ass.

"Hola, flaco, como son los cojones?" *Hello, skinny, how are your balls?*

"El secreto. Ensename el secreto para ganar." *The secret. Teach me the secret to win.*

He puts his arm around my shoulders and draws me close, a fatherly hug. What the hell's wrong with this guy? Get away from me! His strength surprises me and so does the smell of his aftershave lotion. Not Old Spice. Something foreign, lemony smelling, different. Some lusty Spanish smell that attracts girls. That must be it; the Castilian's secret. If I wore that aftershave lotion, girls would like me too.

"Sangre. Sangre es el secreto." *Blood. Blood is the secret.*

"Que? Sangre?" *What? Blood?*

"Si, sangre. Se tu puede sacar sangre, tu gana la pelea." *Yes, blood. If you can draw blood, you win the fight.*

"Como? El es mas fuerte, mas grande. Como puedo sacar sangre a el? No puedo." *How? He's much stronger, much bigger. How can I draw blood from him? I can't.*

"Yo te enseno." *I will teach you.* "Los Americanos no tienen estomigo para sangre." *The Americans don't have a stomach for blood.* "Cuando vean sangre, parece que todo es perdido." *When they see blood, it looks like all is lost.*

We move near the boxing ring and he shows me how to put up my dukes, fists chin-high, never blocking my vision, slight crouch, elbows tucked in to protect my midsection and ribs, chin down, one foot slightly in front of the other. He tells me to jab at his face. I flick my hand towards him and let it drop down to my side.

"No. Mira, a si." *No. Look, like this.*

His fist flashes an inch from my nose and instantly back in position near his chin. Twice more, he snaps his fist in front of my nose, arm straight out, elbow locked for an instant. He moves to a heavy bag suspended by chains from a rafter near the roof. Argelio reaches straight out and touches a spot on the bag.

"El nariz, flaco, el nariz. Siempre tira a el nariz. Hay mucho sangre por dentro el nariz." *The nose, skinny, the nose. Always throw at the nose. There's lots of blood inside the nose.*

He pounds the bag with several stiff jabs.

PAP! PAP! PAP!

Fast. Hard. Powerful jabs. The heavy bag jerks, jumps and jangles, the chains straining, once, twice, three times, in less than a second. Punches like that could shatter a face, splatter a nose flat and draw torrents of gushing blood. I imagine my fist hitting Dido's face as I punch the heavy bag.

"Ow!"

The coarse canvas burns my knuckles, peeling back a layer of skin. Argelio hands me the leather mittens. I put them on and practice the jab several times with each hand. Since I hit hardest with my right, Argelio recommends that I box left handed, a definite advantage since most boxers fight right handed. He later teaches me to follow up the jabs with a left cross to the face.

Thursday, after school, we practice some more. We climb into the ring and spar. Argelio emphasizes keeping my hands up and not throwing a jab until Dido's nose is within range. No wasted effort. No faking. No dancing around. No talking. No smiling. Nothing. Just focus and fight. Put up my dukes and throw that jab. Snap it. Fire it, again and again. Hard. Fast. Bang. Bang. A rattle snake strike; powerful, direct, straight out and back. Aim for a spot behind his head. Smash the nose. Dido's eyes will water, turn black, and the blood will flow. Victory guaranteed. Dido will never bother me again, ever, the Spaniard predicts. And, as an added bonus, no one else will either.

God, I hope Argelio's right.

Friday lasts forever. The fight dominates my mind. Everyone in school smiles at me. Some even raise their fists like they're going to fight me.

"I'll be there!" they say.

Some look around, make sure no one is looking, and whisper, "Good luck, Fred. I'm pulling for you man, but you haven't got a chance."

The last bell rings. Doom time. I walk slowly towards the Santa Ella cigar factory, very slowly, as slowly as I can. No one walks with me. They give me a wide berth. They're all afraid of Dido, worried that after he beats me up, he'll beat them up too, my friends, so they're staying away from me. My heart beats faster and faster. Inside my empty stomach, two crows flap their wings, fighting to escape.

When I turn the corner, I can't believe the scene. The whole school is packed into the field, kids jumping around for position like a damn carnival midway when the freaks are on display.

Dido is already there of course, smoking a cigarette, smirking and strutting around. He's surrounded by several guys, hoods, probably Marianna reform school buddies.

Argelio sees me. No smile or grin, he just raises his right hand to his waist, makes a fist and nods his head once.

I walk towards Dido and the human circle closes behind me, like a cage in a cockfight.

Center stage, Dido takes off his shirt, wads it up, and throws it to one of his buddies. He warms up by slowly swinging left and right hooks in front of his hairy and muscular chest.

"I didn't think you would even show up, pindejo. But I'm so glad you did," he says as his silver tooth flashes in the sun.

Argelio takes my schoolbooks and places them on the ground. Goose bumps sprout out all over my body. My palms are cold and clammy as I clench my fists.

Everyone's quiet as I stand and stare at Dido who begins to walk slowly towards me. He goes into a low crouch, both fists low, near his waist, face and chest wide open. I put up my dukes, tuck in my elbows and go into my own little crouch, just like Argelio taught me.

Dido stops, looks at me, stands up straight, and starts laughing. He points at me.

"Look at the maricone," he announces to the crowd. "He thinks he's a boxer. Ha, you think that scientific shit is gonna help you? Just wait till I hit you one time, you maricone."

Dido's smile vanishes. He crouches, moves several steps towards me and my right fist snaps out and back. He jerks his head back. No contact. His eyes open wide in surprise for a split second. Back into his crouch he moves towards me again.

Snap! Snap!

I throw the two jabs so hard the button on the end of my long sleeve shirt pops off and flies into the crowd.

Dido backs off, stands up straight and sneers at me for a long moment. Glancing at his friends, who are cheering him on, Dido comes at me again, faster this time, with more resolve, closer.

My next jab barely reaches the tip of his nose.

We pause.

A breeze blows across the field. Dido's friends suddenly hush. I touched him with that jab. I can feel his snot on my knuckles, wet and cool.

Dido stands up straight and feels his nose. Then he sticks the tip of his thumb and index finger inside each nostril.

Bleed, I pray to myself, *bleed like a damn faucet.*

His friends are shocked. Everyone is quiet, watching Dido, waiting for him to pull his fingers out and look at them. Dido looks puzzled and his long eyebrow furrows as he stares. The tips of his fingers are bright red with blood, just a little blood, though, not the rushing torrent I prayed for.

First horror, then anger crosses his face as he glares at me. A tiny trickle of blood leaks from each nostril. He wipes them away, violently.

"You son of a bitch; you fucking pindejo, maricone. I'm gonna kill you now. You made me bleed. Now you die."

He waits for my response. I keep my dukes up, stare at him, and stand my ground. He forms a claw with his bloody fingers.

"You see these three fingers? I'm gonna grab your throat, squeeze your windpipe and choke you to death, you son of a bitch. You hear me?"

"What? No more boxing? Now you wanna wrestle? Come on," I say.

Suddenly, everyone in the circle starts yelling and running away.

"The cops! Somebody called the cops. They're almost here," someone yells.

Dido's eyes switch from anger to fear. He lowers his face, grabs his shirt, pulls it over his head, and leaves the area, his friends shielding him from view.

Argelio grins, hands me my books and pounds me on the back several times.

"Bravo, flaco. Un poquito sangre gano la pelea por ti." *Hooray, skinny. A little blood won the fight for you.*

Later, my hands still trembling, I ask Argelio, "You're a Spaniard. How in the hell did you know Americans don't like to see blood and don't have a stomach for blood?"

"La corrida de toro, flaco, y el boxeo."

From bull fighting, skinny, and from boxing."

Here's my uncle Joe Langiotti in his prime as a boxer from Tampa.

He fought under the name Joe Miller.

This is how Ma and Dad looked when they first fell in love.

First Love

"Guess who likes you, Freddie. I can't believe some girl actually likes you," laughs my good friend Julio.

"Who! Who likes me. What did you hear?" I ask, my eighth grade interest fiercely piqued.

"Carmen Rodriguez likes you. Her sister told my sister who told me that Carmen broke up with her boyfriend Tino and thinks you are really cute."

I can't believe my ears. This is the first time in my life that anyone actually likes me or even expresses an interest in me. Carmen is a beautiful girl who's been going steady for over a year with an older guy in the ninth grade named Tino, a strong, quiet football player who's very tough.

Red and black crepe paper is strung across the ceiling of every classroom and cheap paper skeletons line the hallways of West Tampa Junior High School. We're celebrating Halloween, 1958. Last year, the Russians shocked the world by launching Sputnik, the first satellite to orbit the planet. All it did was transmit electronic beeps that scared the hell out of the United States. President Eisenhower responded by establishing NASA and pouring millions of tax dollars into our schools to boost math and science. If the commies wanna race us into space, well, we'll show them.

None of that matters to me now. A girl likes me.

It's lunch time and we're in the courtyard between the main school building and the shop so I immediately began looking around for Carmen. I see her talking to her friends, her back to me, looking pretty in her crinolined white dress, white socks, blue blouse, and two-tone shoes. A red bow contrasts with her long black hair that falls below her shoulders.

Running around, pretending I'm being chased by someone, I screech to a stop, positioning myself in her line of sight and just stare at her. Eventually, she looks at me, makes eye contact and smiles. I bolt away and begin running around the courtyard, a new surge of adrenaline mixed with young love, fueling my nervous body, jumbling my thoughts and looking for answers to life's most important questions: *How do I talk with*

this girl? What do I tell her? How can we go out? Will
my mother drive us? Does she want to go steady? and
many, many more.

The next day, alert in spite of not sleeping most
of the night, I walk to school an hour early and stra-
tegically position myself so I could see Habana Avenue
and Cherry Street, her likely avenue of approach.

Finally, I see her walking with two friends, coming
down Habana Avenue, so I sit on the concrete wall that
supports the side yard of West Tampa Junior High
School. I stare at her intently until she and her two
friends can't help but notice me, a hungry vulture
perched on the wall. The two friends peel away and she
and I are face to face. I break the ice.

"Hello. I heard that you like me, is that right?"

"Who told you that?"

"A friend who knows a friend who knows a friend,
you know how that goes."

"Well, I do think you're kinda cute, but I just wanna be friends right now. Is that OK?"

"Yeah, sure. I think you're cute too. I've always thought that. Going steady with Tino, I never told you, because, you know, I don't wanna get beat up or anything."

"Well, Tino and I broke up so don't worry about him."

"Great! Can I have your phone number? I'll call you and we'll talk."

I memorize her phone number by mentally repeating it over and over.

That evening we speak for more than an hour. My left ear is sweating so badly the phone keeps slipping. No matter how many times I wipe it, sweat trickles down my cheek. We speak every evening of every weekday and two or three times a day during the weekends.

During that first weekend, I ride my bike back and

forth in front of her house for hours, hoping to catch
a glimpse of her through the window or coming outside
and sitting on her front porch. I wish she would see me
and invite me in to sit with her. During the school
week, she spends every available minute talking to me,
introducing me to all her friends, letting me walk her
to class, carry her books and walk her home after
school.

My friends laugh at me. I've completely deserted
them, or "left them flat" as we say. They're jealous so
I ignore them. If they don't understand, the hell with
them.

I treat Carmen Rodriguez with respect and love,
open and honest about everything and she seems to respond in kind. There are some setbacks. She's willing
to go to the Westown Movie Theater, but she won't let
me tote her on my bike. Tino has a car and they used to
go out in style so evidently her days of going out on a
bicycle are over. Unfortunately, it'll be a couple of
years before I can drive the family car by myself.

One Friday morning she asks me if I want to go to

the drive-in theater.

"How?" I ask.

"With my older sister and her boyfriend. She invited me and said I could ask you to come along."

"Great! Do you want me to go to your house on my bike, meet you at the school, or what?"

"We'll pick you up at your house. Where do you live?"

"2703 Nassau Street. The white concrete house with the green window awnings."

"OK, we'll pick you up at 7:45. The movie starts at 8."

The whole day is a dream. At home, my Aunt Mary is in town. She's blond, beautiful and exciting. My mother's sister, Aunt Mary ran away to Miami at a young age to become an exotic fan dancer. I tell Aunt Mary about Carmen, how much I love her and want to go steady, how we're going to the drive-in tonight and about wanting to buy her a going-steady ring. Aunt Mary gives me a dollar bill to spend and says that if I want to ask Carmen to go steady, she has just the ring I need. She opens her purse, digs around for a while and produces a bright, silver ring.

"Here's a nice going steady ring, Freddie. You give this to her. She'll be really happy."

At 7 PM I'm waiting on the porch, nervously pitching back and forth on a green rocking chair, freshly showered and smelling great. I splashed lots of dad's after shave lotion all over my entire body and my teeth are brushed twice for good measure. Finally, I'm waiting for my first date with a girl, the first time in my life.

Prior to this, I had attended dances at Rey Park in West Tampa. Rey Park had basketball courts with steel chain nets, large steel swings, a playground for smaller kids and an outdoor stage where the annual Duncan Yo-Yo contests were held. My dad chaperones the Saturday night dances at Rey Park. My friends and I stand outside the girls' bathroom and wait for a girl to come out.

"Do you need someone to blot your lipstick?" we ask. They frown at us and we bust out laughing, slap our thighs and point at them.

Occasionally, we dance a slow dance with a girl. One night, I was dancing with a girl cheek-to-cheek and gradually, I began to slide my lips along her cheek towards her lips. Usually, at this point, the girl pulls away and frowns, often refusing to dance with me anymore until the next week.

Well, this girl didn't back off and I'll never forget her. Her name was Lucy DeDiego. I moved my lips closer to hers until we're actually kissing, lip to lip. I couldn't believe it! I was really kissing a girl. After a few moments, I opened my eyes, pulled my face back and looked at her. She smiled. My whole body was electrically charged with sexual energy.

After the song was over, I had to walk around with my hand inside my pocket, holding down my penis and thinking about something else to try and ease the raging erection threatening to rip through my jockey shorts. Thoughts of nuns, priests, confession, making a genuine act of contrition and the pains of hell were ineffective. Nothing worked.

Rocking on my porch, just thinking of kissing Lucy again causes a stir in my loins and a "cheating on her already" feeling of guilt as I wait for Carmen so I mentally try to change the subject. Walking to her car with a boner in my pants seems like a bad way to start our first date.

Promptly at 7:45, their car pulls up and all three of them are sitting in the front seat. The car's a four door, so I get into the back seat behind the driver and Carmen gets in behind her sister. We each sit near our doors, as far apart from each other as possible. She makes the introductions and I say "Hi," immediately forgetting their names. I just stare at Carmen as she converses with them. Unbelievable. We're going to a drive-in theater for the night where they usually play several cartoons and two movies, ending around midnight. To add to my luck, the driver guy pays for all of us so my dollar bill stays in my pocket.

We pull up the hill next to the speaker pole and he positions the car so we can all see the screen. He raises the window an inch or two and sets the speaker on the top edge of the glass inside the car. Then he turns the volume up loud so we can hear the music. The sun goes down, the sky becomes darker and the coming attractions start to play. Then two short cartoons and finally the first movie begins.

Carmen's sister slides across the front seat until she's right next to her boyfriend who remains behind the steering wheel. I motion to Carmen to slide down to my side and she motions for me to slide down to her side. As a girl, she should do what I want. I shouldn't have to do what she wants. We motion to one another several times, each time with more emphasis.

Finally, she breaks the silence.

"If I move over there, we won't be able to see the movie because their heads'll be right in front of us," she says.

Unable to break the logic of that statement, I slide over to her side and we hold hands, my right hand in her left hand.

In front of us, her sister starts making out with her boyfriend, kissing him long and hard on the lips, moving around to his neck, around his ear, back down his neck and finally back to his mouth.

That must be why Ma and Aunt Mary call it 'necking,' a lot of kissing on the neck.

Their hands are hidden so I assume they're just hugging each other tight. The hell with watching the movie, I'm enthralled and excited by the action in the front seat.

Thankfully, wearing two pair of jockey shorts helps keep my pecker in place and absorbs any fluids that might escape. So far my strategy is working well.

Suddenly, I remember Aunt Mary's ring in my pocket. I pull it out and show it to Carmen.

"Would you like to go steady with me," I ask.

She says yes and takes off the gold chain around her neck, strings it through the ring and puts the necklace back on. The ring slides right into the middle of her powdered cleavage, the outline of her bra visible under her blouse.

"Fred just asked me to go steady and I said yes," she announces to everyone as she turns towards me and kisses me on the lips.

"I was waiting for you to ask me to go steady. I wasn't gonna let you kiss me until you did," she whispers to me.

"Well, I'm glad I did," I respond and kiss her again, and again and again.

I try kissing her neck and then her ear lobe, one eye on the guy in the front seat, copying what he's doing. Carmen seems to enjoy this so I keep kissing her, going back to her lips often. Once I kiss her so long I nearly faint because I'm holding my breath. Breathing through my nose, I learn how to keep our lips in contact and still get air.

A strange thing happens.

While I'm kissing her, she opens her lips slightly and her tongue comes out and touches my lips, flicking left and right. A renewed jolt of electricity zaps through me, a direct line of energy from my lips to my penis pulsing strongly against the two layers of cotton holding it in place. I jerk my head back and look at her.

"Do you like that?" she asks. "You try it."

Kissing her with open lips, my tongue goes out and meets her tongue and once again, the electric surge is so intense I'm ready to explode. She kisses my neck and moves up to my ear, sucking the lobe, biting it gently and flicking it with her tongue. She sticks her tongue into my ear and probes deeply, over and over.

I explode--four powerful throbs!

Fortunately, all the sticky mess is absorbed by my undershorts.

Everything she does to me, I do to her. We keep all our clothes on and our hands never touch each others' privates.

Every time I try to slide my hand onto her breasts, she says no. Unbutton her blouse--no. Touch her knees and move my hands up her thighs--no. We just kiss.

All four of us in the car are breathing heavy now and as the October night becomes cooler, our windows fog up so heavily that rivulets of water are running down the glass.

Startled, we hear the sounds of car motors as they leave. The last movie had ended.

My body for the last four hours has been in another dimension, an elevated level of sensitivity so strong that my brain is foggy and I'm unable to think. For hours, strong feelings have leaped between me and Carmen like bolts of heat lightning jumping from one storm cloud to another.

The driver guy grabs a towel from beneath his seat, wipes the front windshield and the two side windows and then throws the towel back to me so I can wipe the back windows. He starts the car and drives me home.

In front of my house, Carmen gives me a goodnight kiss.

"I had a great time, Freddie," she says. "Maybe we'll do this again sometime."

I thank her sister's boyfriend for paying my way into the drive-in and realize we never went to the snack bar for a soda or pop corn, or pizza or anything. The entire four hours were spent necking.

My knees buckle slightly when I get out of the car and I almost fall down. Staggering onto my front porch I sit alone for a while before going inside.

In my room, my pants slide off OK but my jockey

shorts are glued together, damp and sticky. I throw them into the trash can and cover them with paper, planning to sneak them into the wash when my mother isn't looking.

Things go well between Carmen and I for two more weeks until she calls me one Friday afternoon after school.

"Fred, I've got something to tell you. I'm breaking up with you," she says as my jaw drops open. "Tino asked me back and I want to be with him, so we're breaking up."

"Why? What did I do?" I say as tears fill my eyes. "I thought things were going great. I love you and I thought you loved me. Why are you breaking up with me?"

"I told you. Tino wants to get back together with me. I want to be with him, not you. So we have to break up."

"But we're going steady!" I yell. "I gave you a ring. You wore the ring to school, every day, around your neck. Everybody knows we're going steady. I told my friends. What am I gonna tell them now?"

"I'm sorry, Fred," she says and pauses for a few moments. "I'll give the ring back to you Monday. It's in my purse. I gotta go."

"Wait! Can I come over and see you? Can we go to the drive-in one more time? Let's talk about this before you break up?"

She doesn't answer so I continue.

"Why? What did I do? If I did anything wrong, I'm sorry. I won't do it again," I plead. "Just tell me what I did wrong and I swear, I promise, I won't do it again. Please."

"You didn't do anything wrong, Freddie. You're a sweet kid. A nice guy. I just like Tino better, that's all. I gotta go. We're going to the drive-in tonight and I gotta get ready. Goodbye."

Click. The dial tone sounds loud and painful.

With the phone still in my hand, I begin to wail so loudly and with so much pain that my mother comes running.

"What's wrong, Freddie?" she asks. "Did you cut yourself? Are you bleeding? What happened? What did you do?"

"Nothing, Ma! Leave me alone!"

The pain of being broken up with for no good reason is so shameful I can't admit it, even to my mother. In the movies, love always looks so happy. How could this hurt so much?

I run to my bed and dive face down, crying and sobbing. My pillow absorbs my screams and the hot burning tears flowing from my eyes. My three younger sisters are afraid and stay away from me for weeks. Joe, my one-year-old brother and roommate wearing only a diaper, stands up in his crib, his big brown eyes staring at me. He recognizes my pain and agony. All through the weekend, I remain in bed sobbing every time I wake up from short periods of fitful sleep.

Early Monday morning, I sit on the same concrete wall of West Tampa Junior High and wait. Carmen walks up to me and hands me a crumpled tissue.

"What's this?" I ask.

"The ring."

I carefully unwrap the tissue, revealing a tarnished brass ring, not the bright silver one that I had given her.

"There's something wrong," I say. "This isn't the same ring. The one I gave you was shiny bright and silver."

"It's the same, Freddie. It wasn't real silver. It was silver plated and turned. It was a cheap ring, pretty on the outside, but ugly on the inside."

She walks away.

After school I watch her and instead of walking

home, Tino pulls up in his car. She gets in, kisses him on the lips and they ride away. I never speak to her again and I swear that no one will ever hurt me again as badly as she did.

Julio joins me on the walk home from school.

"She broke up with me, Julio. I didn't do a damn thing wrong. I can't believe it. We were doing so good together. I don't know what happened."

"I know what happened, Freddie. My sister told me. Carmen never liked you. She always liked Tino. When Tino broke up with her, she went out with you to get Tino jealous. She used you, man."

"No, that's not true. Nice girls don't do that. She liked me, man, I know she did. And I love her. I still do."

"You may love her," Julio laughs, "but she likes Tino. Not you."

"Fuck you, man. You're jealous!"

"Forget her, Freddie. She played you for a sucker. My sister tells me that's what girls do. Nice guys like you, they play for suckers. Don't be stupid, man. Come on, let's go shoot some baskets."

"No, you go. I can't, man, I'm going home. I'm hur--I mean I'm just too mad right now. See 'ya."

Aunt Mary Langiotti in Miami, 1934

Throwing Eggs

In May of 1959, I'm a 9th grader and even though I'm
fourteen years old, access to a car is no problem.
These are the days before social promotion and Junior
High School is 7th, 8th and 9th grades. If you don't
pass the 7th, you have to repeat the whole year. Many
of my fellow classmates have repeated 7th grade once,
twice, some even three times and it's not unusual to
have 17-year-olds in school waiting until they're 18
and can legally quit school to work full time. Some already have part-time jobs and use school to catch up on
their sleep. Some date and impregnate their younger fe-
male classmates. Most have fun just beating the crap
out of us younger kids every day.

Weighing barely over a hundred pounds, my friends
call me "Biddy" because my legs are so skinny. They
compare me to the bright-colored baby chicks sold before Easter time and when I come around, they make
"peeo, peeo" sounds with their mouths. My hair is short
and flat, as flat as my Dad can cut it. My soft, fine,
hair never looks stiff like the brush-looking hair my
friends sport.

Once, when I went to Angelo Rumore's barber shop, I asked the barber to cut it extremely short and flat. Angelo refused.

"Why?" I asked.

"Because your head has too many lumps," he replied.

Now I feel doubly embarrassed because not only is my flattop not as flat as everyone else's, I wonder if they could see the lumps on my head. I've never heard of a barber refusing to cut someone's hair short because of head lumps.

Even though I'm very skinny, wiry and strong for my size, I'm still no match for the majority of my schoolmates. Constant teasing gives me a sharp tongue and I can quickly embarrass others; however, that doesn't stop them from teasing and harassing me mercilessly, even to the point where tears and fists begin to fly.

Since both my mother and I are color-blind, I often go to school with one navy blue sock and one black sock. My trousers never match my shirt and I often commit some other standard dress code violation that invites ridicule. My clothes are never new and are often torn from playing sports, wrestling or fighting with others—another tempting target for ridicule.

Taking my first public shower with other students after gym class is an eye-opening experience. Coach Urso mandates that everyone must buy a jockey strap to wear under our gym shorts. "A peanut and rubber band" he jeers and laughs. We also have to bring our own towel. The shower is mandatory--no excuses. Changing into gym shorts I use the wall locker door as a shield to hide behind. I quickly remove my underpants, step between the thin jockey straps, get tangled, stumble to my knees, recover and immediately pull my shorts up over my bare butt. Then we go outdoors for football, basketball, volleyball, or whatever sport is in season.

Afterwards, coming in all sweaty and dirty, getting naked and walking into the shower with others for the first time is a visual, cultural and physical shock. Most seventh graders my age have no pubic hair or body hair and our penises are tiny and thin. Those who are a bit overweight or chubby look even worse because their penises are hiding under an awning of fat.

Then the 17 year-olds come in with their well-defined muscles, chest hair and pubic hair all thick and curly. Their huge penises, lolling limp and long, become semi-erect when they lather their crotch areas with bars of soap to make foamy white suds. They love wrapping one hand around the base of their soapy penises, sliding it up and flicking a foamy white dough-nut onto us younger guys and laughing.

One short guy, Joe Alvarez, always masturbates in the shower. His penis is huge, more than nine inches long and has a distinct curve to the left. Everyone calls him 'Little-Joe' and since he always uses his left hand to jack off, we figure his penis adapted by curving to the left.

Coach Urso walks around with a wooden paddle and if he catches any of us pissing in the shower, he smacks that paddle on our bare butts, leaving a bright red welt, a perfect paddle imprint that includes small pink circles matching the air holes he drills near the end of the wooden paddle.

"Reduces wind resistance," Coach Urso explains the holes. "When I swing real hard, I can make it whistle too."

Little Joe jerks off in the corner of the shower, constantly looking over his left shoulder, left hand pounding his piston back and forth. When Coach Urso walks through the shower area, which he frequently does, Little Joe quickly raises both hands up to his head and makes believe he's washing his hair. Then he turns his body slowly, keeping his back between Coach Urso's eyes and his swollen pecker, now bobbing up and down, waiting for Coach to leave.

"Hey you guys, look here," Little Joe announces, both hands behind his head, fingers interlaced. When anyone looks, he makes his dick bob up and down like a construction crane lifting a load. In the shower, we always give Little Joe and Coach Urso plenty of room. I pretend not to see him jacking off every day yet I secretly watch, excited by the possibility of Coach Urso catching him in the act. I also wonder if I'll ever measure up, be a real man like Little Joe. I pray that my dick'll grow that big someday.

Near the end of the school year, me and Tony Buggica convince Joe Castro, who has a car, to take us out throwing eggs.

Tony is short, stocky, strong and brutal. He still combs his hair with a part on one side. Tony never gives up trying to train his hair into a pompadour with a duck-ass or DA in the back. DA's were the in thing for cool guys, flat tops for jocks or athletes, and Tony still wore what we called the "little boy" haircut. His face has huge cheeks always flushed red like he'd just been in a fight. When he does fight, which is often, he leads in with his face, his fists low, down by his waist. Tony lets you hit him several times before he throws vicious left and right hooks that are extremely punishing. When he speaks, spit flies out of his mouth and dribbles down both sides of his lip. He starts every sentence with, "Hey, man." Always laughing and making fun of others, Tony is sometimes slow to realize when we're making fun of him. Then his smile turns into an open gape. When he gets really pissed, his lips press together, his eyes narrow into thin slits and his hands go down to his sides, balled into tight fists. Most of the time, Tony is a lot of fun. He loves to go out throwing eggs, firecrackers and cherry bombs.

Joe Castro is our perfect driver. Quiet and serious when sober, Joe wears glasses with thick black plastic frames that make him look like an egg-head honor student. He was the West Tampa Junior High's quarterback in the 8th grade but is ineligible his 9th grade year because of his age. Joe's a good driver and never lets the boisterous behavior going on in the car distract him. He drives a 1949 Ford with a flat-head six cylinder engine. When Joe revs up and pops the clutch, the back tires yelp. Then he speed-shifts into second and finally third gear, making the engine whine and strain. Joe takes corners faster than most cars, slams into second gear, gas pedal to the floor and pops the clutch, spinning the rear tires. Every time he does this, Joe flashes a smile that quickly disappears into seriousness, as if his father is watching. Joe's dad comes to every game and criticizes his every play, loud and insulting. Joe's head and shoulders always slump when he hears his dad.

After telling Joe how much fun we have throwing eggs on foot, he decides to take us in his old grey Ford.

When word gets around, over ten people want to go with us. We narrow it down to six because that's what the car can hold without sitting on each other's laps.

Richard Tribunella gets selected. Richard is short with thick, black, curly hair trained to flow back over his ears without sticking out, a perfect DA in the back. His pompadour on top is over three inches high. Instead of making him look taller, it gives him a black-haired Woody Woodpecker look. The front curl hangs high into the air and dangles in front of his forehead four inches away. His face, ravaged by severe acne, bleeds profusely after a fight, making him look like he loses even when he wins. Richard is always ready to fight. His family moved to Tampa from some-where around New York city and they talk different than we do.

On the first day of school, Richard's prancing around like a little rooster at a cock fight. We over-power him, tie his belt to the flagpole chains and hoist him twenty feet into the air. He's screaming and a huge crowd gathers as we try to lift him higher. We stop when the flag pole bends ninety degrees, lowering Richard down just above the ground, suspended and swinging, butt in the air, cursing us at the top of his lungs. We laugh and run away before teachers let him down. Unfazed, Richard ignores our hazing, dishes out a lot of his own and we soon become friends.

Tony Buggica's best friend, Sammy Villarosa is also picked. Sammy is about five-foot eight, stout and quiet. He lives next door to Tony and stays to himself most of the time. Sammy seems more mature than all of us and doesn't participate in the daily teasing we in-flict on each other. He's always in the background, smiling and enjoying the interaction. He's happy to go out with us because he knows we're gonna have fun.

The final person is Peter Lopez, the coolest guy in school. Pete is short, a little stocky, almost chubby, olive skinned, perfect pompadour and DA, hair never out of place and always sports a heavy gold chain with an engraved image of the Virgin Mary around his neck. Pete never wears tee shirts, preferring pullover shirts with the collar turned up behind his neck. The smell of Old Spice aftershave lotion surrounds Pete for five feet. His Cadillac smells like Old Spice and he always keeps a bottle in the glove compartment, right next to his condoms. His room in his house smells like Old Spice, with several open bottles on top of his dresser and new packages inside his drawers. Pete has a round face, large cheeks, and small lips that are shaped like an archer's bow. I often wonder, because his mouth is so small, if he uses a teaspoon for soup and a child-size fork for other food. But, oh how the girls love those tiny lips and mouth. When we go to a dance, my friends and I greet girls with a hello or a handshake. Not Pete. A big hug and a kiss, right on the mouth as we stare in jealous fascination.

Pete's dad is always home and when we ask why he never works like the rest of our dads, Pete says his dad is a big shot in the dock workers union. The double garage of their house has been converted to a small boxing gym with a speed bag and a heavy bag suspended

from the rafters with chains. Pete's dad was a boxer
and his brother, Pico, is a boxer and also active in
the union with his dad. They all drive Cadillacs, keeping them outside the garage.

One morning, Pico gets into his car, turns the key,
and the Cadillac explodes, blowing off both his feet at
the knees. We never again ask about Pete's family and I
stay away from his house.

Pete's girlfriend, Maria, is the most beautiful
girl in school. Maria has long black hair, black eyes,
a beautiful figure, dresses well, and is very nice,
even to egg-heads, jerks, and people like me. She's
taller than Pete and we marvel how he gets such beautiful women to kiss him and even more.

Maria broke up with Pete over some argument and
when Pete heard we were going out throwing eggs, he
came to us with a special request. He would buy the
eggs if we would bomb Maria's house. We also have to
deny that Pete went with us or had anything to do with
it. He gives us the same excuse for not taking his Cadillac. Maria would recognize it. Of course, we agree

with Pete's plan because eggs are about twenty-five
cents a dozen, very expensive to someone like me whose
allowance is twenty-five cents a week.

Friday evening finally comes and we pile into the
car. Joe Castro is driving, Peter Lopez riding shotgun
and Richard Tribunella is between them, his tall Woody
Woodpecker hair whipping left and right, excited as he
follows the conversations. In the back seat, Sammy Villarosa is behind the driver, I'm in the middle and Tony
Buggica is on my right. We leave the parking lot and
plan to go to a grocery store that stays open late on
Friday nights to get the eggs. Then we're off to Ybor
City and Maria's house.

I have one cherry bomb that I was saving for a special occasion just like this. Cherry bombs are so powerful they could blow both ends of a metal mailbox completely off. Once we put a cherry bomb under an empty
tomato paste can and the blast peeled the can into four
pieces like a banana, spinning it high into the air
like a lawnmower blade. Cherry bombs have wire fuses
that, once lit, cannot be put out. You could flush a
lit cherry bomb down a toilet and it would still ex-

plode, destroying the fixture and spewing water in every direction. We heard one guy lost three fingers from a cherry bomb so when we throw them, we don't waste any time. As soon as the fuse lights, we toss it. The fuses, however, could be tricky because they're covered with a light coating of wax. When you hold the match to it, the wax ignites and quickly burns down towards the cherry bomb's body. This causes tremendous fear. People often throw the bomb prematurely and they don't go off. It's cowardly, embarrassing, expensive and stupid to toss a cherry bomb at someone and then not have it go off. When the fuse properly ignites, it hisses and spews smoke like a small rocket. From that instant, you have about six or seven seconds to toss it, much like a hand grenade. I pull the cherry bomb out of my pocket.

"Hey, you guys, I've got a cherry bomb. Let's throw it at somebody!"

Everyone in the car becomes silent.

Tony Buggica, "Hey man, yeah, let's find somebody walking and throw the cherry bomb at 'em. Yeah."

"I thought we were going out throwing eggs," Joe Castro says, adding quickly, "OK, let's do it. Who's got matches? Do you need the cigarette lighter?"

"I've got matches," I say, "Tony can light it, I'll hold it and I'll throw it out the window. Man, this is gonna be fun."

We turn off Columbus Drive and drive down some back streets until we see a guy walking on the sidewalk. Joe slows the car. I hold the cherry bomb in my right hand, and Tony strikes the match and holds it to the tip of the fuse. Peter looks over his left shoulder, lips in a small 'o.' Richard Tribunella can't decide which way to look and strains, first over his right shoulder, then over his left. Joe watches the road and Sammy stares down at my hand, his eyes glittering like a lit spar-kler. The guy walking on the sidewalk glances at our car, notices that we've slowed down, and sees the match flame illuminating our faces. He stops walking and stares, puzzled by six guys in one car, all looking down into the back seat.

Tony, holding the match, begins to laugh. His whole body shakes up and down. So does the match. I hold the fuse in the flame, moving the cherry bomb up and down and and then I start laughing too. Villarosa, to my left, doesn't laugh, but I can see his eyes gleam with excitement. Joe alternates looking at the road and then back at us. Peter's fixated by the flame and Woody Woodpecker's hair whips left and right. I get the false light first and my heart pounds. I'm not laughing anymore. The wax burns down to where the fuse is glued to the cherry bomb's body. I fight my fear and the strong urge to throw it now, forcing my hand to hold still, keeping the fuse steady in the match's yellow flame.

Finally, a burst of sparks, a hissing sound and a steady spewing of smoke and sparks. I elevate the lit cherry bomb up near the roof of the Ford and twelve eyeballs are riveted to the sight. The only sound is the Ford engine's flat-head six, idling down the road. After waiting an extremely long two seconds, I whip the cherry bomb across my body, directly in front of Sammy's chest, towards the open window. All eyes follow the hissing flame. The cherry bomb strikes the center post between the front and back door windows and fiery sparks fly. The cherry bomb bounces back down onto the floorboards beneath our feet.

"Shit!" Joe Castro screams, "get that fucking thing out'a my car!"

"Pick it up, quick!" Peter yells.

Tribunella's head is whipping around so fast, his movement's a blur. I'm amazed his neck doesn't snap like one of Nana's chickens when she kills it for dinner.

All three of us in the back seat get the same idea at the same time. We stomp our feet without looking down, afraid the bomb'll explode. We stomp left, right, front and back, pounding each others' feet trying to put out that damn cherry bomb. I don't know who started screaming first but now all six of us are screaming at the top of our lungs.

"YAAAAAAAA!"

BOOM!

The car fills with thick smoke. A loud ringing sound shrills my ears. I'm in a silent movie. Peoples' lips are moving, but I hear no voices. Arms, legs and hands are thrashing wildly, eyes shocked, wide open in fear as we stumble out of the car, coughing, choking and cursing. Porch lights come on. We cough our lungs clear, rub our eyes and look at the car. The back floorboard is burning, flames a foot high. Joe Castro shields his face with his forearm and pulls out a burning burlap sack, slams it down on the street and stomps the fire out.

The guy on the sidewalk, our intended victim, laughs and points at us. We run towards him and he runs away.

"Stay with the car," Joe Castro yells and we all stop, go back and evaluate the damage. Fortunately, the back seat did not burn. After a few minutes, the summer breeze clears away the smoke.

"I've called the cops on you boys," one neighbor yells, hiding behind his screen door.

We all climb back in the car as Joe turns off the headlights hoping to hide the license plate number and we roar off, turning the corner on two wheels, tires screeching until we're going straight again.

"Is everybody all right?" Peter asks. "We still gotta get the eggs and bomb Maria's house.

Everyone agrees and soon we're getting out in front of a market filled with shoppers. Pete opens his wallet and takes out a ten dollar bill.

"Everybody get three dozen eggs each!" he says.

When we get to the register, the clerk, an old country man, looks at us, smiles, and asks, "Whut you boys cook'n with all them eggs?"

"We're gonna make an omelet," I reply, "a big omelet."

We all laugh. Inside the car, storage is a problem. We have eighteen dozen eggs and nowhere to put them. We stack some behind the back seat, some on the dash board, some on the floor, and everyone keeps a dozen or two on our laps. Even Joe, while driving, doesn't want to miss out on the action. We're armed and ready.

Peter tells Joe how to get to Maria's house and we cruise past several large homes in an old well-kept neighborhood.

"That's it, the house with the white steel bird on the screen door," Peter finally says.

Joe stops the car and we all get out.

"Hey man, you want us to start throwing now or what?" Tony Buggica asks.

"Call her," Pete whispers, "and as soon as she opens the door, blast her. I'll teach that bitch never to break up with me again."

After saying that, Pete crouches behind the front door so he can't be seen.

"Maria!" Tony yells. Then Joe Castro and I join in, "Maria! Maria!"

Richard Tribunella, always trying to out-macho us, runs across the sidewalk and into her front yard until he's just a few feet from the door.

"Maria! Maria! Come out here, Maria, we wanna see you!" he screams in his New York accent.

I'm tempted to pelt him with an egg just to get the action going, but I hold my fire.

The porch light comes on and Richard runs back to the car. We each have one egg in our throwing hand cocked behind our heads waiting for the screen door to open. We wait for over a minute.

Peter, still inside the car, whispers loudly, "Call her! Call her again."

We all started chanting in unison, "Maria. Maria. Maria!"

The chanting reminds me of Catholic High Mass and I think of the Virgin Mary medal Pete wears around his neck. What we're about to do is a sin and even though the excitement is irresistible, I feel badly.

My uneasiness started when Peter referred to Maria as a "bitch." This girl was always nice to me and not many girls are, especially those who are beautiful and know it and flaunt it around school. My conscience screams, *Speak up for her, Freddie. She's a nice girl.*

These thoughts vanish when the screen door opens and a woman with long black hair peers outside.

That's all we need. A target. We open fire. Three eggs splatter all around her head, hitting the door, the wall, and the steel bird frozen on the screen. Tribunella's egg flies over the top of the door, exploding on the spanish tile roof. My egg hits the woman in the forehead and I see the white eggshell shatter and imbed itself in her hair. The yellow yoke streaks a blond stripe on the top of her head. We're laughing uncontrollably. We grab egg after egg, throw 'em, then more. The woman screams, shuts the screen door, slams the front door, and turns off the porch light.

I pee my pants.

We bolt back into the car, Joe puts it in gear, pops the clutch, the back tires yelp and we speed off, squealing around the corner.

"We hit her mother!" Peter yells, "That was Maria's mother! She didn't even come out, dammit. Let's go back and call her again!"

"Hell no," I say, "the cops'll be all around here soon. Joe, slow down, dammit. Everybody calm down. Man, I pissed my pants that was so funny."

"Let's go back," Pete yells, "Maria was probably just inside the door. We can go back and call her out again."

"Hell no," I yell back, "we can't risk it, Pete. Joe, drive normal like nothing happened."

My mixed feelings return. I feel bad for intending

to attack a beautiful girl who was nice to me and re-
lieved we splattered her poor mother instead. I shoot a
guilty remark at Peter.

"Besides, Pete, she's probably out on a date," I
say. "It's Friday night and no girl as good looking and
nice as Maria'll be home on a Friday night."

Pete looks gives me a serious look, eyes burning.
Everyone becomes quiet, anticipating a fight. I fanta-
size about a Friday night date with the beautiful, sincere and sexy Maria.

We drive around in silence for twenty minutes, coming down off the adrenalin high. We spot a young man
wearing a suit and tie walking down the sidewalk.

"Let's egg him," Richard says. "He's going to a
dance or something. Look at him. So special. First
date, wearing a coat and tie. . . what an asshole!"

We circle around the block, eggs up and ready. We
creep up behind him, slowly and quietly. He's walking
on our left, on the driver's side and before we're

alongside him, we start throwing.

Peter sticks his right arm out the window and hooks an egg over the roof of the car, splatting the back of the kid's suit jacket. To my right, Tony Buggica tries to copy Peter but his egg splatters the roof of our car, yellow yoke oozing down the back window. Joe Castro and Richard Tribunella fling eggs through the driver's window. Another egg, I don't know who's, hits the guy on the back of the head. White eggshell slams into his duck-ass haircut, disappears, and yellow yoke runs down his neck and back. Sammy, in a furious display of agility, flings six eggs so fast they look like a train, connected and evenly spaced as they arch towards their target. Three hit and three miss.

My egg hits the post between the front and back window, exactly where the cherry bomb hit. The egg explodes inside the car. Yoke and shell spatter Joe Castro's neck, Sammy's shirt and the car's cloth-covered ceiling. Throwing three more eggs in rapid succession, no one notices my misfire. No one even notices they were hit by my egg.

The victim never looks at us. He just lowers his head, does an about face and starts walking back home, probably to phone his date, change clothes, take a shower and try again later when this carload of crazy nuts leaves the neighborhood.

Whooping with laughter, we describe what we saw.

"He just turned around and left! What a pussy!"

"No balls! Didn't even look at us! Or throw us a bird!"

"We fucked his date! Wait'll his mother sees him!"

I laugh so hard, tears stream down my cheeks. We continue to drive around. The guys toss an egg once in a while at a stop sign, a billboard, a car going in the opposite direction, and, when we wait at a stop sign, at a dog sitting on the front porch of a house. The dog jumps up, startled and puzzled, looks around, sniffs the spattered egg and licks the unexpected treat.

"Hey man, lets go to the projects and hit some jiga-boos!" Tony says. "That'll be fun, man."

"Good idea, Tony," Tribunella pipes in. "Let's do it Joe, come on. We're only a few blocks away."

"Yeah, let's do it, Joe," we chime in and soon we're patrolling the projects of Ybor City where poor people live.

The streets are deserted and all the porch lights are off. This seems unusual for ten o'clock on a Friday night.

"Where's everybody at?" I ask.

"Inside fucking," Richard says. "That's all they do. Fuck and have babies."

Segregation is the law in 1959 and the Negroes or 'colored people' as we call them, have their own schools, their own neighborhoods, playgrounds, hotels, restaurants, bars, restrooms, drug stores, night clubs, whorehouses and even their own water fountains. On Sundays afternoons, about twenty or thirty of them come into Macfarlane park to play football against us Latinos. We play rough tackle football, no helmets or equipment and end up with bloody noses, sprained ankles and the occasional broken arm or collar bone.

In Tampa's social hierarchy, Anglos act like they're at the top, followed by the Spanish and Italian on a somewhat equal level with each other and then the Negros. Homes and school books are transferred down the same line. From Anglo to Latin to Negroes.

Some Latinos with Negro features insist they're Spanish and trace their history back through Cuba all the way to Spain. Others claim they're indigenous natives or 'Indios' as they call themselves. It's a standing joke among Latinos and even Anglos that whenever we see a beautiful Negro girl, we always say she isn't black, she's Indio or Indian and this earns social approval for our desire to date her. Of course, it's against all our beliefs. Convention mandates that we date and reproduce only within our own race, nationality and culture. Latinos are treated like distasteful subhumans by the Anglos, though not as badly and openly as they treat the Negroes. Like the coloreds, Latinos refer to Anglos as "crackers" and we speak Spanish in front of Anglos to make them feel uncomfortable, giving them a taste of their own discrimination whenever we can.

We know that throwing eggs at Negroes may upset the false harmony and thin veneer of peaceful coexistence but the issue of macho courage overshadows social concerns.

Besides, this is really fun and we want more.

Turning a corner, we see a car with four old black women, all dressed nicely and wearing hats like they're just returning home from a church social or wedding reception. They're traveling in the same direction as we are, right in front of us and we decide to bomb them. Joe pulls out to pass their car and when we get alongside them, he holds that position while we prepare to pelt them with eggs.

When we stay alongside their car, the driver glances at us and the first egg hits her right in the face. Peter, Richard, Tony and I fling eggs out the passenger windows directly into their car less than three feet away while Joe and Sammy shoot awkward left-handed hook shots over the top of Joe's car. The women scream as eggs disappear into their open windows, smashing against them and the inside of their car.

Unbelievably, I pee my pants again.

We stay alongside them. The driver comes to a complete stop and so does Joe. Their screaming is so loud we can't make out what they're saying. We laugh and enjoy the slaughter, hurling dozens of eggs at their vehicle.

Behind us, headlights in high beam flash like double spotlights. I turn around and look. The car speeds towards us, accelerating quickly.

"Joe, let's get out'a here," I yell. "A car's coming!"

Joe looks back. So does Richard, Pete, Sammy, and Tony. Twelve eyeballs, looking through our back window through the yellow and milky-white slime. Several eggs roll around the back window ledge, still intact. Miraculous.

Joe tries to lose the car now hot on our tail. He turns left at the first street, right at the next and races towards Columbus Drive. The car behind us catches up and our bumpers are close. His bright lights blaze into our eyeballs as we take turns looking back at him.

Just past a corner filling station, Joe squeals right at the next turn. The car behind us cuts across the empty filling station and a vacant lot, narrowly missing a pump. Both of his rear tires are screaming white smoke. It's a brand new 1959 Ford Fairlane driven by a large white male. His powerful V-8 engine catches us and he cuts in front of us. Joe slams on his brakes. Eggs fly between us and splatter on our laps and floor boards.

In the smoky haze, the Ford car door opens and out steps the biggest white man I have ever seen. He's six-foot-seven, weighs 300 pounds and he's carrying the longest and brightest flashlight I've ever seen.

He shines the light into our car as he walks towards us. Our eyes are drawn to the light and he blinds us. I squint and shield my eyes with one hand.

"I'm Detective Sergeant 'Tiny' Anderson, Tampa Police Department," he says, search-lighting our front seat. He shines it on Joe, then Richard, then Peter. Moving to the back seat he points the light at Tony, me and Sammy. Then he shines the contents of our car-- dried egg yolk on the back window; broken eggs on the floorboard; eggshell in our hair; dried egg on the posts between the windows; and several egg splatters on the roof.

"You boys been out throwing eggs?" he asks.

"No sir! No sir," we answer in unison. "We haven't been throwing eggs."

"Bullshit. The whole car looks like a fucking omelet. Now, everybody get out. Stand against the car with your hands on the roof. I saw you blast those old ladies."

We get out, close the doors and stand facing the car, hands on the vehicle as he checks each of us for weapons by patting us down with one hand while holding the flash light ready, like a huge silver hammer, to bash us if we make a wrong move.

Traffic on Columbus drive stops. People stare at us, watch the event unfold in front of the filling station, a giant white man with a huge flashlight, searching six young guys, hands hugging an old '49 Ford.

"What are you gonna do with us?" Joe Castro asks.

"Well, the first thing we're gonna do, is go back there and see if those ladies are all right."

"Please don't take us back there," I say. "I'm sorry we did it. I apologize. Can you just let us go? We won't do it again, I swear. Come on, please."

"No, I can't let you go. I want you to see what you did, face to face, to those ladies."

"Hey man," Tony says, "you're a white guy, just let

us go, man, we won't do it again."

"What if they come out and beat us up," I add, "can you protect us?"

"Everybody back in the car. Don't try to run," he says. "You saw how fast I caught you, so no funny business. Follow me. I'd put you all in my car but there's too damn many of you and I don't wanna get raw egg shit all over my brand new car."

"We'll wash her car for a week, Officer," I plead, trying one last time. "Just don't take us back there, please. We'll take turns for a year. A whole year, each of us. That's six years. We'll wash her car for six years."

"No good. Now lets go," he says.

We climb back into Joe's car and follow the detective in his unmarked car back to the scene.

"That fucking cop won't let us go because he's a cracker. He's the biggest fucking cracker I've ever seen," Peter says on the way back to the scene. "You know why the bastard's taking us back to the projects? So when they beat the shit out of us he can stop'm and be a hero."

"Oh shit," I say. "Let's stick together. Don't get out of the car unless we have to. Roll up the windows and keep quiet. Oh God, I hope we get out'a this without getting our asses kicked."

When we get to the scene, he pulls alongside their car and gets out to speak with them. We all stay inside Joe's car, watching.

"Dat's them, officer, them's da boys that done it, dat's them!" the women yell as they point to us.

Using small white handkerchiefs with embroidered edges, the women dab their faces and foreheads trying to sop off raw egg residue. Their car is completely spattered, inside and out. A couple of eggs hit their hood and one even hit the left front hubcap. Porch lights string both sides of the street and people gather in a large semi-circle around the victims, all facing us cowering in our car.

We sweat. The windows are rolled up tight. The raw, broken-egg stench gets stronger and stronger.

Get us out'a here, God. Please, get us the hell out'a here! Man, what's wrong with that cop? Can't he see these people are gonna kill us. They'll skin us alive and eat us for breakfast!

Finally, the detective comes over to Joe's window and taps on the glass with his giant flash light. Joe cracks the window slightly.

"Follow me to the station house," the cop says. "I'm gonna book you all."

Joe follows him downtown. As soon as we leave the projects, we roll down our windows and breath a sigh of relief. The warm night air cleanses some of the raw egg smell from the car.

"Dammit," Joe says, "my father works at the police station. He's the guy who checks people in when they've been arrested. He'll beat my ass right in front of everybody."

When we get inside the station, two uniformed officers walk towards us.

"Joey, what are you doing here?" one of them says.

As the man walks closer to us, he notices the egg yolk and egg shells in our hair and clothes.

"Oh, you used your car to go out throwing eggs, huh?" He puts his face right in front of Joe's and yells, "I ought'a beat the shit out'a you right here and now, God damn it. You get into that cage like the rest of your monkey friends."

We're herded into a small cell and asked to give our name, age, address and phone number. Because Tony is 18 years old, he's taken into the back and jailed with a bunch of drunks, as he tells us later.

A policeman announces that we have to call our parents to come and get us.

"Can I just spend the night here?" I ask, afraid of what will happen when my father gets a hold of me.

"No," he says. "Everyone must call and get picked up tonight. I'll have your court date and papers ready before your parents get here. You first," he says, pointing to me.

It's past midnight as I dial my phone number. After several rings, my mother answers.

"Hello, Ma," I say, "Can you pick me up and give me a ride home?"

"Sure Freddie, are you OK? Where are you?"

"I'm OK, Ma. I'm at the police station."

There's a long pause.

"Ma? Can you come and get me?"

"Your father will come and get you."

Click.

I stand there with the receiver stuck to my ear,
listening to a loud dial tone for several moments as
the cops watch me.

"OK, Ma. Thanks," I say to the buzzing sound and
hang up.

"Oh shit. Oh shit," I keep repeating as I plod back
to the holding cell. "He's gonna beat the living crap
out'a me."

We finish our calls and Richard Tribunella's parents arrive first. They speak with the police officers,
fold up some papers and watch us, a deadly serious look
on both their faces. Richard walks towards them.

"Not here, not here," Richard's mother warns, one
hand restraining the center of her husband's chest.

"All right, all right," he responds, voice rising
before turning phony and pleasant. "Come on Richie.

Walk in front of me. The car's right outside, heah."

His mother leads the way, then Richard, then his
father. As Richard reaches the door, his father can't
restrain himself any longer. He glances around to see
if anyone is watching and slaps the back of Richard's
head as hard as he can. Richard sprawls out into the
street, arms flailing, as he tries to keep his balance.

*That's what dad's gonna do. That's EXACTLY what
he'll do.*

Waiting in the cage, I differentiate between
smells--raw eggs, floor wax, bleach, sweat, Old Spice
and the steel-cold smell of fear.

When my dad walks in, he looks white like the blood
has drained from his body. He speaks with the cops,
folds sheets of paper and jams them into his pocket.
Now he stands inside the doorway waiting for me to
pass--his favorite attack position. When he comes home
from work and hears from Ma the horrible things I've
done to aggravate her, he calls me in from outside, positions himself in the doorway and, when I walk past

him, starts the beating by slapping the back of my head just like Richard's father did to him.

Once, I refused to walk past him.

"I won't hit you," he said. "Now come in. Hurry up, before I come out there and get you. If I have to come after you, it'll be worse. I promise you. Now get in here, God damn it!"

Of course, I didn't believe him. But the fear of "it" being worse compels me to enter the house, ready to duck, anticipating the blow to come.

Now he's in that same position. He'll hit me in front of all these cops.

Maybe the cops even expect it. Shows them what a good parent Dad is; that he supports their efforts to stop crime in the streets and a good beating will do just that--act as a deterrent to future crime, making their jobs easier. Hell, they'll thank him for beating me in front of them so they can be a witness to it, enjoy it, maybe even breaking out into a cheer after-

wards, followed by a round of applause.

I walk towards him and he looks at me like I'm a complete stranger, some kid who doesn't belong to him, someone he's picking up at the police department as a favor to some poor mother and the court papers are part of the administrative details involved with helping out a neighbor, a kindly act, expected from religious people like Dad.

In a burst of speed, I duck through the doorway, shocked that there's no blow to the head, no foot kicking my butt, no razor strop whistling through the air. I turn around, puzzled and stare at Dad.

"Just shut up and get in the car," he says and I do it.

"You scared the shit out'a your mother," he adds on the way home. "We don't know what we're gonna do with you but I'll think of something."

When we get into the house, we sit around the kitchen table, Ma, Dad, and I. Mom has been crying and finally she speaks to me.

"Freddie, I hope you never do anything like this again. Next time, we'll leave you in jail until you rot. We won't get you out, Freddie, you hear me?"

I nod my head and we all sit quietly for several minutes. My dad jumps up.

"I know what I'll do!" he says.

He opens the refrigerator, takes out an egg and cracks it over a coffee cup. He lifts up the white shell and shakes it until everything globs into the cup. He slams the cup down in front of me.

"Drink it. Drink the whole damn thing until there's nothing left," he says. "Go out throwing eggs, huh? I'll show you. Drink that now!"

I lift the cup to my lips, slurp the egg into my mouth and swallow. It tastes like slime. I gulp and swallow several more times until nothing's left.

"Now go to bed," Dad says and that finishes the night of throwing eggs.

The court appearance results in a verbal warning from the judge about throwing things from cars. He remarks that some kids threw a grapefruit at a man riding a tractor, the man fell off and the tractor ran over him, killing him.

Since that night, I've done many exciting things but nothing has ever resulted in me peeing my pants twice in one night.

I feel older now, more mature, like I've crossed some invisible line between adolescence and adulthood. Kids get spanked. Young adults get punished. Maybe I won't get beaten anymore, ever again. I ponder this and pray for it to be true. I also decide that some actions and emotions, even though they are extremely exciting and fun, just have to be kept under control.

This is the plaque in front of the Macfarlane Park swimming

pool dedicated to Baldomero Lopez, United States Marine

Corps Medal of Honor winner during the Korean war.

What Happened to Lastra's Pharmacy?

I was jubilant in the early 60's and my first job at Lastra's Pharmacy, 3133 Grand Central Avenue in Tampa, fueled my optimism.

Teresa DiMarco prepared Lunch Specials, a meat dish that always tasted Italian. Waitresses Betty, Mary and Solie served television personalities like Channel 13's Hugh Smith, Salty Sol Fleischman and Andy Hardy as well as kids my age who came in to talk about girls, sports, Elvis and the Beatles.

Behind the counter we walked on wooden slats and every Saturday morning, I'd carry them out back, hose them down, sprinkle them with Ajax and scrub them with a stiff brush. When I rinsed them, the bleached wood was fuzzy-white and clean.

"Nobody cleans those slats like you do, Freddie. Keep up the good work," Mr. Lastra would always remark and I'd swell with pride.

Arthur Lastra, the owner, coached Pony League baseball at North Palomino. He was easy to spot because he wore a safari hat instead of a baseball cap like everyone else. He loved sports and let me off work for all my games.

John Lastra, one of Arthur's three sons and a football and baseball star at Jesuit High School and the University of Florida, also worked in the Pharmacy. John's laughter boomed throughout the store and his clipped sentences were part of his charisma.

"Hey, Freddie. How many you strike out Saturday? Still lost, eh. Too bad. You ain't worth a damn. You hit? Good. Gain some weight. Malted milk; every day. Put eggs in it. Double the hamburgers. Eat, man. You too damn skinny."

Linda, John's girlfriend, worked the front cash register. One day she came in wearing her Catholic school cheerleader outfit and smiled at me. My first girlfriend had broken up with me so I was crushed and her smile restored my hope. Now I had a crush on Linda so I found any reason to go up front under the guise of helping her. I asked her advice about girls until I saw John and Mr. Lastra glaring at me. John could have crushed me with one hand so I slunk away.

Mrs. DiMarco found out about my girl troubles and suggested I talk to Mr. Morgan, a steady customer.

"He's very wise," she said. "Wait on him for a few days and then ask him about girls. He'll teach you."

Old Mr. Morgan, hunched over at the waist, hobbled in every morning dressed in a suit and tie. He wore thick glasses with heavy black frames; his hair was thin and reddish-white and his long-sleeved shirts were always starched. He shuffled into the drugstore, painfully settling onto the same stool every day and ordered the same breakfast.

Soon, when I first saw him outside through the plate glass window, I started preparing his breakfast and had it served by the time he settled onto his stool: Two eggs, sunny side up; four strips of bacon, well done; grits; two slices of whole wheat toast slathered in butter; and a cup of hot black coffee.

One morning, as food steam fogged his glasses, he smiled at me so I decided to lean over and talk to him.

Solie taught me more than just cooking. She taught me timing. Today, I'll ask him about girls.

"Mr. Morgan," I whispered and leaned closer, pained, like I was in a Catholic confessional. "My girlfriend broke up with me. Mrs. DiMarco said I should ask you about girls. How do I pick a good one?"

"Freddie, Freddie," he frowned, "I'll tell you all my secrets, free of charge. But first you gotta wait till I finish my breakfast."

Twenty minutes later, he lit up an unfiltered Pall Mall, inhaled deeply and blew smoke towards the ceiling. After a few moments, he looked left and right for privacy and leaned forwards towards me.

"Freddie, if you want to know how your girlfriend's gonna look in the future, look at her mother. If her mother's fat, she'll be fat too. If her mother's skinny, she'll look the same. You wanna know how she'll treat you? Look at the way she treats her brothers and sisters. If she screams at 'em and is mean to 'em, you can be sure you're in for the same thing. If she loves them and treats 'em nice, you know you've found a good one."

"What if she's an only child?" I asked, puzzled as I tried to absorb his wisdom.

"Look at how she treats her pets. If she loves 'em, she'll love you too. If she mistreats them, you're in for it."

"Sir, how'd you learn all this?" I asked.

"Freddie, I'm eighty-nine years old. I've kept my eyes and ears open and my mouth shut. That's the way you learn, son. Experience. Mistakes. Starting over again--from scratch. People race by me today; knock me over trying to get ahead. They never ask my advice. I gave it to you because you asked."

One night, my friend Dwight Ferguson came into the drugstore with a stranger, a tall, skinny kid.

"Freddie," he announced, "I'll bet you this guy can eat three of your banana splits."

"No he can't, man. My splits are huge," I answered. "No human being can eat three. Tell you what. If he can, I'll pay for 'em. If he can't, you pay me double what they cost—a dollar each. He's gotta swallow every bite or you pay. Bet?"

"You're on, Freddie," Dwight said as we shook hands. "Start making those splits and make one for me while you're at it."

I peeled a banana, split it and laid the pieces in a long, boat-shaped glass bowl. Then I hand-dipped three huge scoops of ice cream, chocolate, vanilla, and strawberry, and pressed them between the slices. Next, I poured a full ladle of chopped pineapple, swimming in sticky syrup, over the vanilla scoop; a full ladle of strawberries, stewing in their own juices over the strawberry scoop; and then I pressed several long squirts of hot chocolate syrup over the chocolate scoop. I sprayed whipped cream over everything until the three mounds were covered, deep and white. Then I sprinkled crushed nuts and topped everything off with a long-stemmed cherry. I slid the bowl in front of the kid and made a duplicate split for Dwight.

Both guys devoured every drop.

I made the next banana split for the kid even bigger, spilling precious juices over the edges of the
glass boat. The kid took longer, but he finally finished the second one.

"Well, you give up?" I asked him. "I don't wanna
waste another split on you if you can't eat it all. You
look full."

The kid stared at me without saying a word.

"Fix'm the last one," Dwight said. "And prepare to
lose."

The third banana split was titanic. When I finished, ice cream overflowed around all the edges of the
glass boat and dripped onto the counter. The kid cast a
fearful glance at Dwight, then started eating.

An hour later, the guy swallowed the final drop. He
managed to hold everything down and sat there droopy-
eyed, inebriated by the huge sugar overdose.

"Well sucker, you just lost three hours worth of
work," Dwight laughed as I jammed a dollar-fifty of my
own money into the cash register.

In 1963, John F. Kennedy's convertible passed in
front of Lastra's Pharmacy on his way to the Tampa Air-
port. Thousands of people, responding to his message
about the torch being passed on to a new generation,
lined Grand Central Avenue just before his flight to
Dallas. Young and old cheered and waved, unaware we
were saying goodbye.

The next year, still motivated by his words, I
picked up that torch, joined the Marine Corps, volun-
teered for Vietnam and was wounded twice in what later

proved to be a lost cause after American troops left and congress cut off their funding.

Today, Grand Central Avenue is Kennedy Boulevard. I miss people like Coach Lastra, Mr. Morgan, Theresa, Betty, Solie and Mary; I wonder where John and Linda are now and how Dwight and that skinny kid are doing.

Drugstores no longer have soda fountains and tables filled with friendly people, but whenever I walk into one, I still feel compelled to look around.

"Can I help you, sir?" the cash register clerks usually ask. "Are you looking for something in particular?"

Yes, I am," I reply. "But I don't think I'll ever find it again."

Joe and Marian; Nina and Arthur Lastra being served by Betty.

Wayne Bright, Us Against Them

"Time Out!" Coach Rimoldi yells. He walks out to the mound and takes the baseball away from our pitcher. Back on our bench, we relievers worry. Who's going in now?

It's 1961 and our Jefferson High School is beating Hillsborough, 7 to 5, bottom of the last inning. Roy Carrasco, tired, has somehow managed to fill the bases and there are no outs. We're playing for the Tampa city championship.

We have to win. It's more than just a game. Jefferson versus Hillsborough is Latinos against Anglos; spics against crackers; the poor against the rich.

Hillsborough's kids buy new baseball gloves and spikes every year. Jefferson players rub olive oil to revive old gloves and sharpen rusty spikes with a file. Hillsborough's school district is 95% Anglo, Jefferson's is 95% Spanish and Italian.

In the segregated South, we had "white" and "colored" bathrooms, water fountains, restaurants, neighborhoods and churches. Black schools could only play against each other. The effects of segregation and prejudice, however, were more widespread.

Although Negro, Spanish, Cuban and Italian cultures and languages are different from each other, the Anglos grouped us together as one minority group. We also lumped them together into one pot, no matter where their ancestors emigrated from in Europe.

Coach Rimoldi looks at his relief pitchers: Bruno, Rabada, Palmeiro, Tomasello and Bright.

"Bright, get in there," Rimoldi barks and tosses the ball to the lefty.

Coach's voice is high-pitched from the tension and pressure that causes most human throats to constrict and give rise to the word we never utter out loud to our teammates--*choke*.

We frown at each other, puzzled.

What the hell's Coach doing? He's putting in a cracker and a sophomore to face Hillsborough's top three hitters with the bases loaded and no outs.

From the first day Wayne Bright came out for base-ball, we mocked him. Wayne had bright red hair, blue eyes, red freckles and was six-foot-three, one-hundred-and-fifteen pounds. We called him "carrot-top" and "pencil with a red eraser." We held him down and tried to play connect the dots on his arm with ballpoint pens.

"Hey Red, who pissed on your head?" we'd yell and he'd always reply, "the same son-of-a-bitch who crapped on yours."

When we were around Wayne, we always spoke Spanish to make him feel uncomfortable. We all agreed he had big *cojones*, but we never told him.

On the mound, Wayne kicks a small pocket on the left side of the pitching rubber and starts his warm-up tosses.

Batting against Bright was like facing a giant praying mantis. He had a high knee lift and a long stride towards the plate. When he delivered the ball, his left arm swung down below his waist and behind his back. Then he swung his hand towards first base before flinging the ball home, what we called "sidearm," closer to "submarine". His fastball was slow, but it tailed away, never in the same direction. His curveball broke sharply in the opposite direction and dipped downwards.

Coach hated to let Wayne Bright throw batting practice because we cracked so many bats trying to hit against him. The wood shattered in your hands and the stinging pain swarmed through your forearms like thousands of high-voltage wasps.

Tonight, the cracker Wayne Bright has to face Dennis Luneberg, Mac Farrington, and the traitor J. J. Fernandez, whose family somehow survives living in Hillsborough's area.

The fans packed into Cuscaden Park are screaming, half for us, half for them. Horrible, shameful names fill the air, hurled equally from both dugouts. Wayne presses his freckled lips together and fires his first pitch. Luneburg swings and misses. All three runners are waving their arms and screaming at Bright, trying to distract him. They take long leads off their bases, ready to run as soon as the batter hits the ball. Dennis Luneberg grins with confidence, taps the bat against his new spikes and digs in deeper. Two more vicious cuts and Luneberg's out.

Mac Farrington, their star quarterback, takes three mighty swings, misses every one and sprints back to the dugout, a frown on his embarrassed face.

J. J. Fernandez takes a called first strike, fouls one off and misses his final swing with a loud grunt, followed by a violent scream as he slams his impotent bat down on home plate and cracks it in two. Game over.

We explode out of the dugout, hoist Wayne onto our shoulders and parade him in front of the grandstands.

I adopted Wayne Bright that day. He was one of us from then on. For the first time in my life, I thought *maybe some of these crackers aren't so bad after all.*

Baseball at Al Lopez Field was big in Tampa!

NGS ARE
T FIRST!

It was the biggest crowd since 1957 at Al Lopez Field to watch the Yankees and Reds play with 5,672 customers paying their way in. These kids, however, apparently didn't have the funds to get in and climb the light tower to get a better view but . .

Ralph Lavandera and Nellie Fox's Bat

        Whenever I think about Ralph Lavandera, and
I've thought about him a lot over the last 50 years,
there is one incident that epitomizes Ralph's character
and summarizes why Ralph is where he is today.

        It happened in March of 1960 inside Tampa's sold-
out Al Lopez Field, the only baseball stadium that I
know of in our country's history where the namesake,
Hall of Famer and Tampa native Alfonso Ramon Lopez,
born on August 20, 1908 and died on October 30, 2005 at
the age of 97, outlived the physical structure dedicated to him. The stands were filled to capacity that
day with short-sleeved, white-shirted fans watching a
spring training game between the Cincinnati Reds and
the Chicago White Sox.

        "I'm gonna take Nellie Fox's bat," Ralph announced
during the 7th inning stretch, surprising us to such an
extent that we just stared at him, speechless, our
mouths agape.

        That simple, declarative statement, spoken by any
other of my friends at the time would have resulted in
a *yeah, sure* response. But Ralph said it, and when
Ralph Lavandera said something, everybody listened.

        The four of us who were hanging out at the stadium
that day were still teenagers; me, Ralph, Julio Rosas
and Joey Lavandera, Ralph's brother.

        We were constantly on the move during the game be-
cause we had no seats. We had no seats because we had
no money and could not pay to get in. Devoted baseball
fans like us never let a small thing like money stop us
from seeing our major league heroes.

We had jumped the fence and were doing our best to blend in among the crowds moving from the first base line, to the area behind home plate, the best spot for viewing the pitcher's stuff, and then to the third base line, staying in the main aisle, walking slowly, pausing often to watch the game, yelling and cheering whenever something happened. We tried to look like four friends going to the rest rooms or to the concession stands, or back to our seats. And for the last hour or so, our ruse had worked well. The game was in the last two innings.

Since Ralph's bold declaration, the frown on his brother Joe's face had been getting deeper and deeper as he thought about what Ralph had said and now, a full five minutes and fifty yards from that fateful spot, he could contain himself no longer

"Ralph, you're full of shit," Joe said.

Julio, who also had been thinking, spoke up.

"Ralph, how you gonna do that? In front of all these people . . . you're nuts, man. You gonna get us arrested."

Ralph's eyes were intense, feverishly focused on the area between the first base line dugout and the on-deck batter's circle. Here, the Chicago White Sox bat-boy had lined their bats leaning against this short fence, single-file, probably coinciding with their batting order. Nellie Fox's bat was the one with the fattest handle, nearly the same size as the barrel of his bat.

Power hitters like Mickey Mantle, Roger Maris and Ted Kluszewski, preferred a thin-handled bat with a fat barrel. When they snapped their wrists during their swing, the bat actually bent a little like a Catholic nun's wooden pointer stick whistling through the air with fierce intensity as she whaled our butts for misbehaving in class.

Just like her stick, right before the moment of impact, the baseball bat would uncoil and explode against the ball with a loud CRACK! The extra speed and power propelled the bat's "sweet spot" against the ball, sending the sphere even further, hopefully over the fence. This whip-action was a scientifically proven fact. We saw it for ourselves in our school classrooms and when we watched slow-motion replays on film and television.

Nellie Fox, however, wasn't a power hitter.

The year before, he was the American League's most valuable player leading the White Sox to the 1959 World Series where they lost to the world champion Los Angeles Dodgers, those bastard "Bums" who deserted Brooklyn by boarding busses in the dead of night, baseball's blatant act of disloyalty signaling to the American public the rise of the dominant almighty dollar in professional sports and that America's real pastime was making riches--loyal fans could go to hell. At the time, I was too young and naive to believe this even though my father swore it was true.

Since little Nellie Fox thrived on singles and doubles, he couldn't care less about whip action. He wanted to extend his bat's "sweet spot" from the barrel as far down as possible, even to his knuckles if necessary, so if a pitcher fooled him with a slider or curve, or jammed him with a fastball, the part of the bat striking the ball was still thick enough to propel the ball through the infield for a hit.

We loved players like Nellie Fox. At 5 feet 9 inches tall and 160 pounds, we had a chance to grow to his size and if Nellie could make it to the majors, then damn it, so could we.

Nellie Fox was a "hustler" and hustling helped make him a star. He never walked or trotted. He ran everywhere, out to his position when the inning started and into the dugout when the inning ended. He bolted towards every ball hit anywhere near his position and ran the bases at full speed even when he knew the ball had popped up and someone would easily catch the soft fly ball. He ran to first base after ball four even when he was entitled to "walk."

A few years later, Pete Rose would say, "hustle is free, it's a gimme" and we already knew what Rose meant. God may not have given us tall bodies, great hand-eye coordination, bulging muscles or blinding speed, but all of us could hustle.

In addition to his hustle and fat-handled bat, Nellie Fox's other trademark was a giant-sized chew of tobacco that so grotesquely inflated his cheek, the eye on that side would squint nearly shut and we were amazed that he could see through what looked like a painful deformity.

Always a league leader in the lowest number of strikeouts and consecutive games played at second base, Nellie Fox was tough and fearless, holding his ground against people sliding into second base trying to break up a double-play, their sharp spikes flashing in the sun, ready to flay open a second-baseman's skin and expose his white shin bone.

Casey Stengel, the manager of the New York Yankees, said of Fox, "That little feller, he ain't so big, but he's all fire. He's caused me more grief than any other player on the White Sox."

And so the stage was set on that bright and beautiful spring day in Tampa when Ralph Lavandera, with declaration and determination, decided to take Nellie Fox's bat.

"What if Fox sees you?" Julio asked. "He could jump the fence, chase you down and beat your ass in front of all these people. I won't help you, man. You're on your own."

"How are you gonna do it?" I asked, as we once again walked down the ramp towards the concession stands. It was the top of the 9th inning. The game was nearly over.

"I've got an idea," Ralph answered. "I'm gonna make it work. Don't come near me when I make my move. If something happens, run like hell. Just stay away and watch me."

I've been watching Ralph from the day we first met in 1957. It was at the Tropical Paradise, an ice cream, soda and snack place in West Tampa on Armenia Avenue near the West Town Theater. On Saturday mornings, we kids would congregate at the West Town for two movies, cartoons, the news and a weekly serial like "Commander Cody of the Space Patrol." It cost us fourteen cents to get in, a nickel for popcorn and another nickel for soda. For that reason, my mother only gave me a quarter. I couldn't beg another dime from her. Forget about asking my dad--he would scream at her for giving me the quarter.

"Freddie, you come straight home after the movie," she'd order me. "Don't go to the Tropical with those dead-end kids. If you hang around with them, you'll get in trouble. You'll end up in Marianna, in reform school."

Sometimes my uncle, who boxed professionally under the name Joe Miller, would dig into his pockets and give me all his change. Whenever he did that, I felt rich. Nearly all the other kids got thirty-five cents from their parents and with the extra dime, they'd go to the Tropical Paradise after the movies to meet, listen to music and talk. I went too and just sat there and watched, broke and a little embarrassed that my parents were so cheap. Many years later I realized we were poor in those days.

One Saturday afternoon, after the movies, I was sitting alone in the Tropical when Ralph and I made eye contact.

"Hey man, come over here," Ralph told me. "Sit down. Have some fries and a Coke? What's your name?"

I introduced myself, joined him and his friends and we all sat together, talking and laughing and having a good time.

Someone at our table finished their soda and when they sucked on the straw, the cup made that horrible grating sound, that brrrraaat-brrrraaat-brrrraaat sound.

A group of girls were sitting at the next table and everyone got very quiet, embarrassed. I don't know if our guys thought the sound hit those girls like a loud fart, or if that type of sound was considered simply rude. To suck a straw so hard against the bottom of an icy cup and make that sound may have equated to picking your nose in public. But whatever the reason, there was an awkward moment that seemed to last forever.

Maybe Ralph's future wife Alice was one of the girls sitting at that other table. Ralph's been with Alice forever, probably since the day she first stood up in her crib, Ralph saw her and selected her as his girlfriend, steady and forever, just like the marriage vows specify, "till death do us part."

The awkward silence continued until, finally, one of our guys, probably Ralph himself, took the initiative to say something.

"God, I hate that sound. It sounds like . . ."

Ralph had started to say what he was thinking and then abruptly stopped, coasted to a halt without a verbal period, like he suddenly realized that what he was just about to say could possibly be even more offensive so he stopped, tried to rethink and drew a blank. This created another awkward silence. His attempt to restore the jovial mood got jammed and the ensuing silence hung in the air.

Suddenly, right in the middle of Ralph's pause, I blurted out.

"Yeah, I hate that sound too. It means you're empty; the soda's gone; that's all there is; finito; you hit bottom; out of gas; sucking air; or in this case, ice."

Everyone looked at me, paused for a moment, and then started laughing, especially Ralph. Conviviality returned to the room and Ralph and I cemented our friendship.

I lived on Saint John Street and Ralph and Joe lived two blocks over on Beach Street. They were a Spanish family dropped somehow behind the Italian lines and were now surrounded by an island of Sicilians.

We ate some sort of pasta every day and had spaghetti sauce three times a week; they ate white or yellow rice every day. Our families spoke Italian at home; theirs spoke Spanish. We were outgoing, loud and boisterous; they were shy, quiet and reserved. Italians knew each other not only by name but also by our Sicilian city of origin.

Ralph's family knew no one at first and we looked on them as those Spaniards from Spain. We kids met regularly at school and on the playgrounds, became friends, fought often and competed in whatever sport was in season. In West Tampa, summer sports were always in season and baseball was king. We played year round, every day.

We rode our bicycles to the baseball diamonds at Macfarlane Park. The first two kids to arrive warmed up with each other and played hot pepper against the backstop. As soon as the third kid arrived, we played baseball using cork ball rules; a batter, a pitcher and an outfielder.

Sometimes we played Home Run Derby, batting from center field and trying to hit the ball over the backstop for a home run. Anything else was an out. When six kids arrived, we switched to modified baseball, picking 3-man teams and using half the diamond. By 10 am, we usually had enough kids to play using the entire field.

There were no umpires, uniforms, or adults to regulate us. We negotiated our own rules, argued, improvised and argued some more. Sometimes we fought with our fists, pouted, made peace, took turns and played until dark. At noon we broke and went to the local grocery store for an RC Cola and a Moon Pie. Then back to the diamond to resume the game. We kept score, often near the hundreds, until kids began to leave for dinner or it got so dark we couldn't see well enough to play.

We did this every day during the summer and every afternoon during the school season. I was going to say "even during winter," but in Florida, winter never stopped anyone from playing baseball. That's why a lot of major league teams came to Florida for the winter.

Baseball equipment was precious to us.

We never threw away baseball spikes. We repaired them with duct tape, needle and heavy thread, shined them with black shoe polish and sharpened the rusty steel spikes with a metal file.

Stiff, dry baseball gloves were resurrected each season, brought back to life by rubbing them with our mothers' olive oil and re-stringing them with shoelaces when the leather cords rotted and broke. We borrowed our mothers' face-powder pads and taped them inside our gloves to protect our palms and dampen the sting of a line drive or hard fastball.

With a ballpoint pen, we'd print our names and phone numbers on the leather and then protect our eyes with two pair of sunglasses as we burned the information in by holding a magnifying glass under the bright sun and tracing the hot dot like a laser over each letter.

Smelling the wisp of burnt olive oil reminded me of cowboy movies and how the smoke from cattle must smell

as their hides were branded and marked for identifica-
tion, a ranch owner's first line of protection against
thieves and rustlers.

This was the era before aluminum or metal composite
bats had been invented and when they were, they far
were too expensive for us to even consider.

Since wooden bats would often crack, we'd take them
to Ralph's house for repair. The Lavandera family had
moved to Bradford Street and their house had a workshop
in the large two-car garage. Like a bone and joint doctor, Ralph would secure the broken bat on his Dad's
vise and get out the glue, small nails, hammer and
tape. Two of us would gently pry open and expose the
crack so Ralph could peer inside and squeeze white wood
glue into the wound, apply pressure with the vice and
seal the wound by tapping small nails into the wood to
keep the crack closed. Sometimes Ralph drilled a hole
clean through the bat and secured the crack with a nut
and bolt, it's sharp edges filed smooth and round.
Ralph was the head surgeon and Joe, Julio and I were
his assistants. We'd leave the bat on the vise over-
night, under extreme pressure, and the next day the repaired bat was released, sanded down and wound with his
dad's sticky black electrical tape until the bat looked
like new.

The thinner the handle, the more difficult the bat
was to repair. One good crack from not keeping the
trademark up when swinging, was all it took to ruin a
bat. We all knew this and maybe that was another reason
Ralph wanted Nellie Fox's bat, a more practical reason
that just happened to coincide with our admiration for
Nellie Fox, our small-statured hero. Nellie's bat would
last longer than the Mickey Mantle or Ted Kluszewski
styled bats. And we needed equipment that would last.

Balls were plentiful. At night, we would climb over the Al Lopez Field fence, jump onto the infield and climb up the backstop screen behind home plate. We were like spiders climbing up an invisible web, three stories high with no visible support beneath our hands and feet.

At the top of the stadium, where the screen joined the roof right above the press box and announcer's station, there was a flat air conditioning panel, a sheet metal barrier that would stop foul balls, trap them and keep them from rolling back onto the diamond or over the roof and onto the sidewalk below. We would salvage between three to ten balls after every game.

If it rained, the balls were soaking wet. We'd take them to Ralph's garage, rub them down with his family's bathroom towels and, using his mother's blow dryer, blast them with hot air until the leather dried and shrunk, stretching the threads and exaggerating the size of the stitches until the covers were ready to explode. After hitting them with a bat several times, these balls would rip apart and if we didn't have any more balls, we'd continue to use them. If it rained during our game, we'd stow our good balls and switch to these water logged, ready-to-split balls.

When someone hit a long fly ball into the outfield, the broken, spinning ball would shed a round rooster-tail of water, like a wet pinwheel, all the way down. When the sun hit it just right, tiny rainbows would appear and disappear just before the ball plopped into our gloves, the sizzling leather flap suddenly silent, like we were holding a deep-fried hot potato.

So, back to that beautiful day at Al Lopez field. The game's just about to end. Ralph warns us again to stay up here in the main aisle. He makes his way down through the expensive box seats towards where the bats are still lined up against the fence. These seats are occupied by rich people who drink huge cups of beer, shell salted peanuts and mindlessly drop the husks onto the concrete ground, not caring that people poorer than us will clean up their mess after every game.

Rich people can afford to take an afternoon off of work and pay big bucks to get in and watch these games. Many even purchased plane tickets and flew in or drove their cars all the way from Chicago or Cincinnati to Tampa, then rented a hotel room and came to watch the game. We could very easily spot these tourists, these Northerners, these "yankees." Their chests, faces and arms were pale and white. They often removed their shirts to get a tan, to try to look like us, we dark and swarthy native Floridians, so sadly outnumbered by them, then, now and forever more.

Ralph saunters down the aisle between these box seats like he belongs there among these people.

He's an outsider, an interloper, one of us. His dark Spanish complexion stands out among the pale people in their white short-sleeved business shirts.

Just as he reaches the fence, the final out is made and the game is over. People jump out of their seats and rush towards the aisles. The players trot off the field toward their dressing rooms, trying to avoid the souvenir and autograph seekers. They're anxious to peel off their sweaty spring training uniforms, hit the cool showers and wash off their sun tan lotion, irritatingly speckled with Florida sand. Then they'll be ready to party long into the night.

God—what a life!

The batboys and equipment managers are gathering up gloves, jars of pine tar, rosin bags, tobacco pouches, canvas bags, jackets and a variety of "hidden" batting helmets starting to make their debut since mandated by the Pittsburg Pirates in 1952. Their heads and eyes are looking down, intent on completing their job so they too can be out of here, onto the bus and headed for their hotels.

That's when Ralph makes his move.

He leans over the waist-high fence, reaches down and grabs Nellie Fox's bat. He lifts it over the fence, clutches it to his chest and turns around with his back to the field. He jams the bat down into his pants behind his belt buckle and slides it down his right pant leg.

Walking up the steps, mingling in with the crowd, Ralph looks like he's got the biggest and fattest boner in baseball history. The long stiffness of the bat down his leg doesn't allow his knee to bend so he goes up the steps with a huge limp, like he's a horribly disabled accident victim, some crippled kid who got to watch the game from the box seats, paid for by some charitable paleface, some rich executive from up north.

Ralph has a faint smile on his face. His eyes are mirthful but there's a touch of fear in there mixed with pride as he finally reaches us.

We break into huge grins. As he hobbles the last few feet, we reach out, catch him and close around him like a glove and shield him as we leave the stadium.

"What balls, man! You did it! You got Nellie Fox's bat!" Julio and Joe are cheering. "Let me see it, Ralph! Stop! Let me see it!"

But Ralph keeps hobbling ahead.

Outside the stadium gate, people are dodging around us to leave, frowning at us when Ralph stops and pulls out the bat. To me, right now, Ralph looks like Sir Lancelot, one of King Arthur's Knights of the Round Table, pulling the huge, heavy and magical Excalibur out of its sheath, holding it up with both hands, taking short choppy swings, careful not to strike any tourists close by who now give us a wide berth.

"Hey, watch it, you kids," they say and walk around us.

We take turns holding Nellie Fox's bat and examining its details. Its 35 inches long, has the fabled fat handle, and it's perfectly intact, no cracks, only a few white scuff marks from hitting brand new baseballs. There's a small dark patch of pine tar just below the trademark and up near the barrel, right on the "sweet spot," we see the famous signature, branded, burned-in and permanent, **"Nellie Fox."**

We used that famous bat for years and if I know Ralph, he still has that bat somewhere in his lakefront house, or maybe at his beach house, hung on a mantle over a pretty but rarely used Florida fireplace, or maybe it's in his office, right behind his desk.

In the 10th grade, Ralph quit school and went to work. Everyone freaked out and worried about his future. We stayed friends and even paid to enter a team in Tampa's Municipal League, promising sponsors we would print their business names on two baseball jerseys if they gave us $25. We were the youngest co-managers in the league.

Then Ralph joined the Army, got out and went to work as a electrician. I got married, joined the Marine Corps and we went separate ways for many years.

Today, Ralph owns Lavandera Electric, his electrical contracting company and is a success story by anyone's standards. He's well known and respected for his diligence, honesty, hard work and his loyalty to his employees.

I admire Ralph for what got him to where he is today--his courage and his focus. The Yiddish call this essential success trait *chutzpah* and the Spanish call it *cojones*.

Ralph Lavandera has them both, by the tons.

And he's got Nellie Fox's bat to prove it.

some bad advance from our pitching coach (Clyde King) and foolishly tried to blow the ball by the hitters.

"I'm not that kind of a pitcher. I'm a changeup guy. Have to fool the big, strong hitters by changing the speed on my pitches.

"That's what I'm concentrating on this spring."

Third Base Problem

The Lopez game also may have settled the question of who will play third base for the Yankees. Will Yogi Berra?

It gets more dubious every day with Gil McDougald effectively handling the chores and Berra doing lusty hitting when he operates at his regular catching position.

McDougald had three hits in yesterday's 13-3 victory, after which Manager Casey Stengel remarked:

"McDougald has been hitting like his old self, which is very good, and he has been covering ground."

A much-relaxed Berra, who has taken a few ineffective turns at the hot corner, had a home run and four runs batted in while playing only five innings.

NGS ARE T FIRST!

It was the biggest crowd since 1957 at Al Lopez Field to watch the Yankees and Reds play with 5672 customers paying their way in. These kids, however, apparently didn't have the funds to get in and climbed onto the light tower to get a better view but . . .

. . . plenty of people wanted to see the Yankees and filled up the entire stadium plus most of the bleachers. Here the first base bleachers are crowded with spectators —(Times Photos by Vernon Barchard).

This is a copy of the 1957 Tampa Times (photos by Vernon Blanchard). The two kids at the back of the light pole watching the Reds play the Yankees are **Ralph and Joe Lavandera.**

Today, Macfarlane Park is the home of West Tampa Little League where thousands of kids hone their baseball skills trying to make it to the "Big Leagues."

Times have changed--they always will.

Made in United States
Orlando, FL
03 April 2025

60117621R00075